METACONTRAST

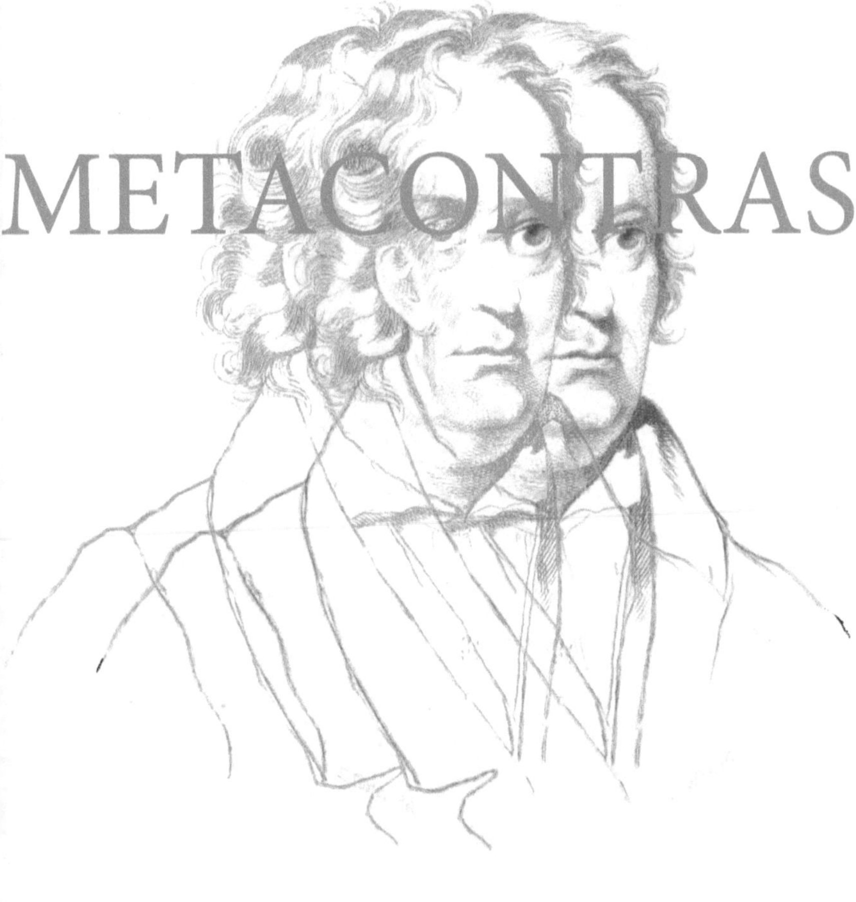

Donald Daedalus

2011

Performer

Artifice

Distance of

Observer

Reaction
(Experienced)]

Observer

Reaction

Resonance

[Experience
Experienced:

Performer

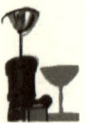

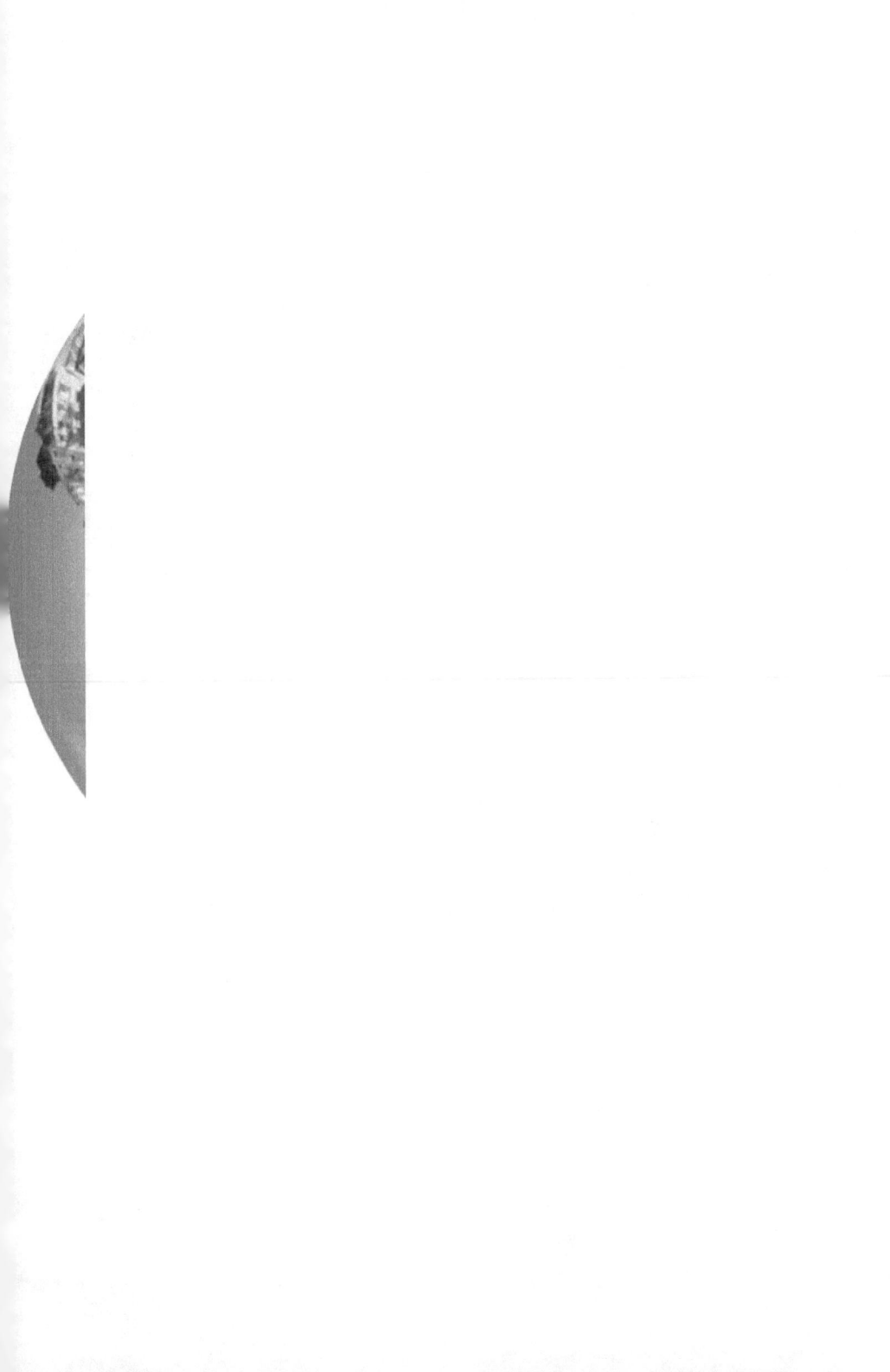

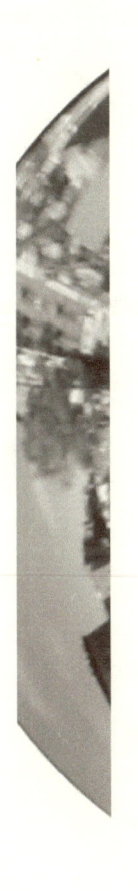

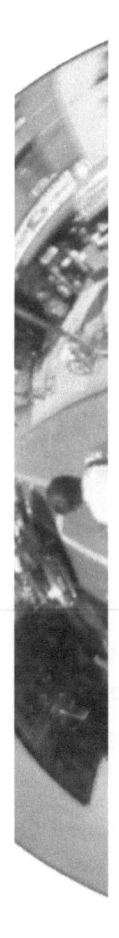

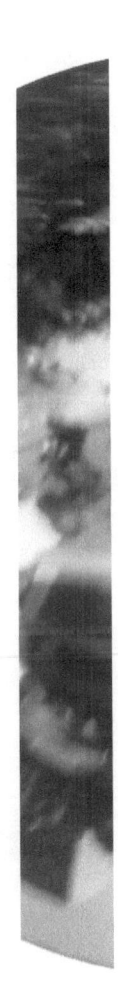

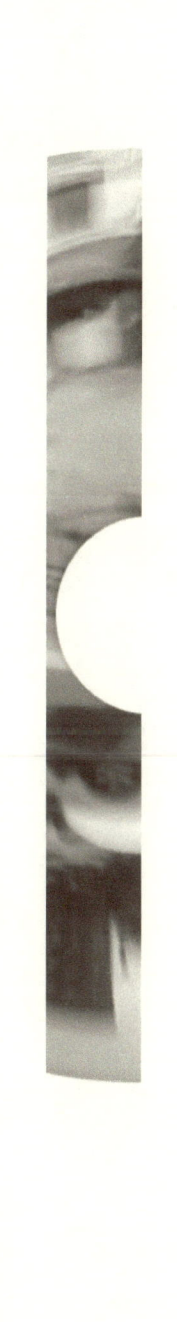

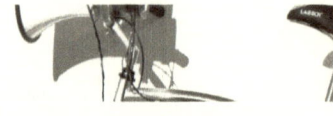 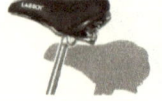 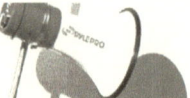

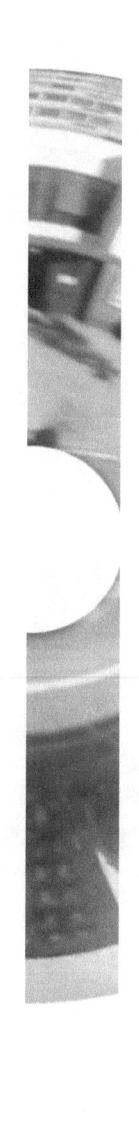

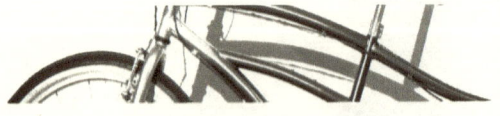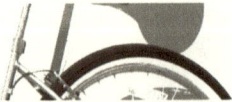

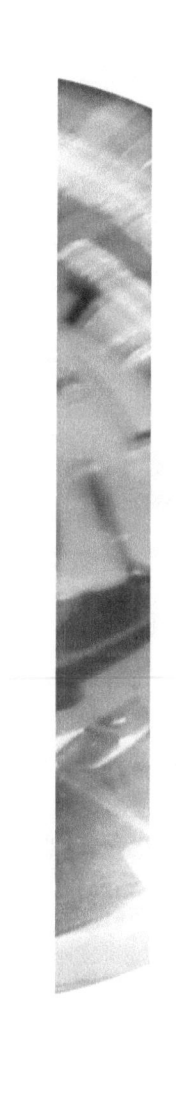

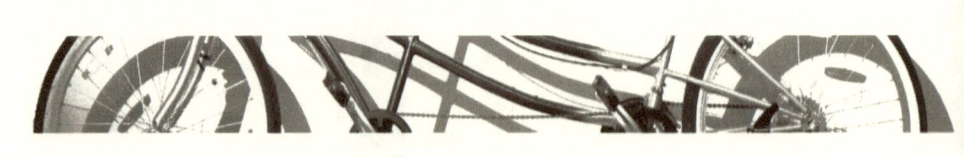

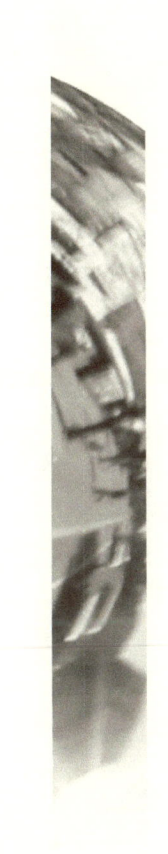

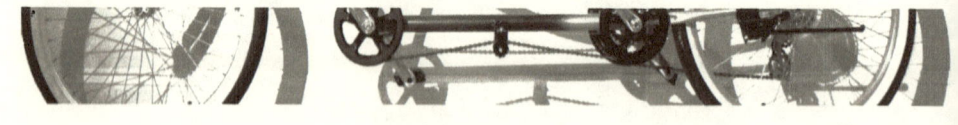

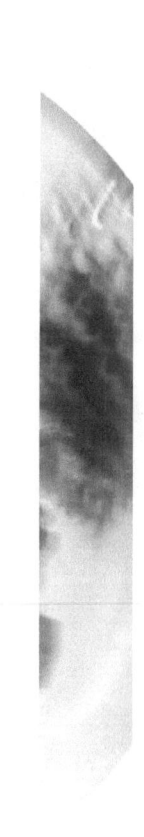

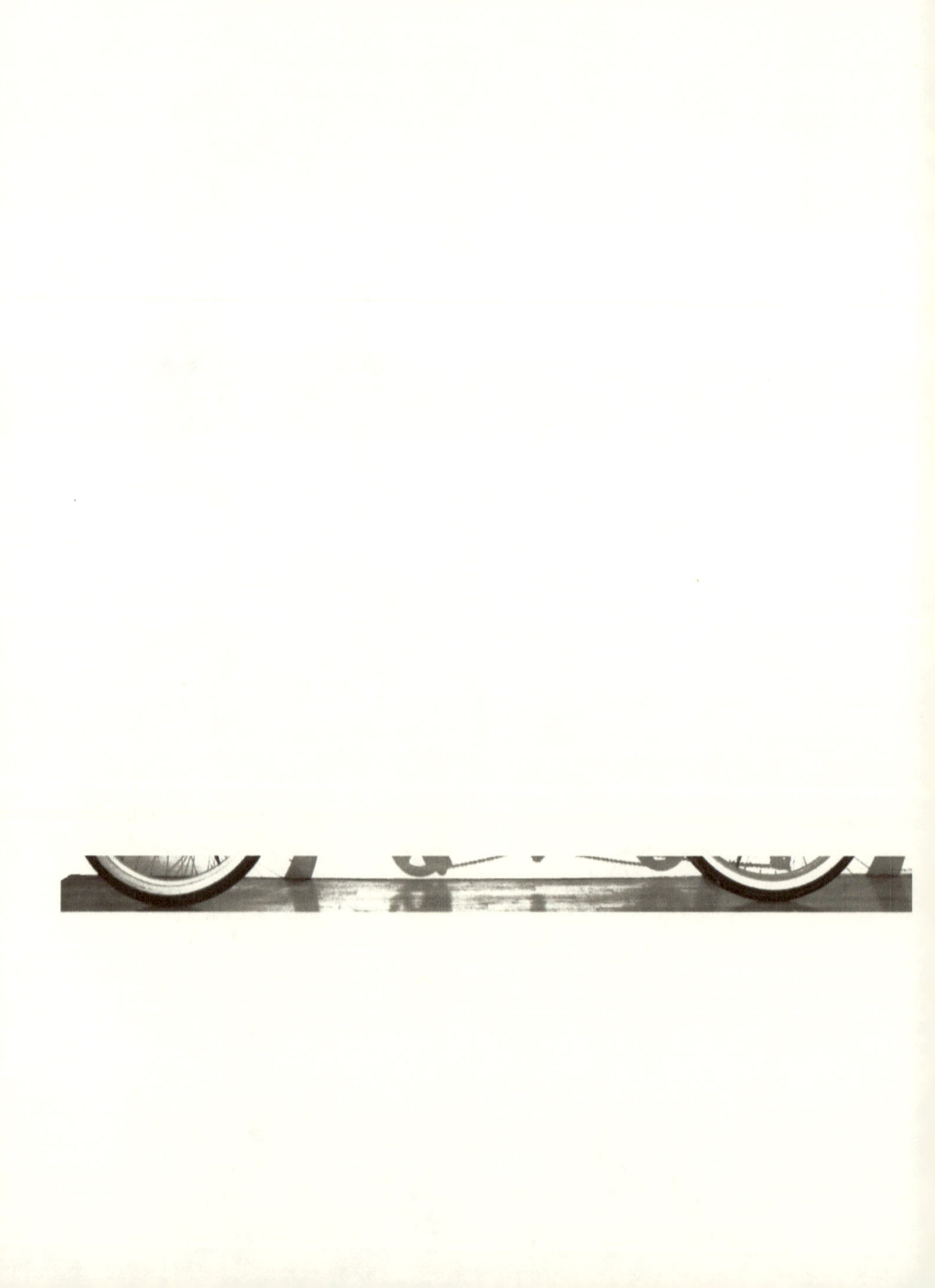

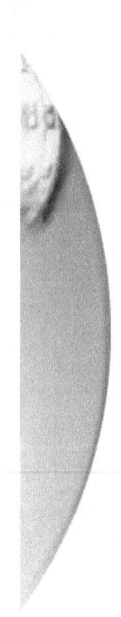

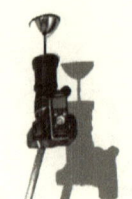

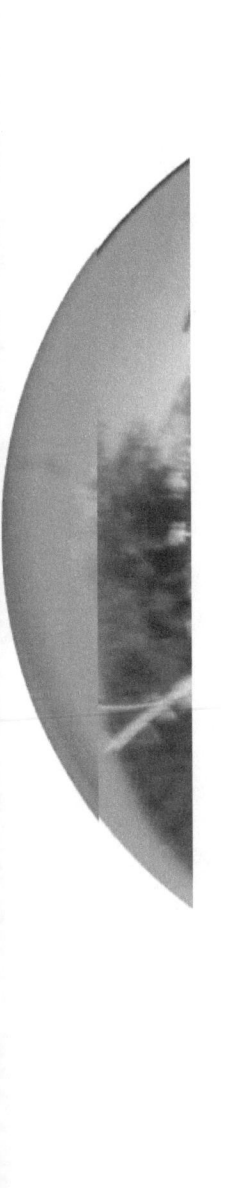

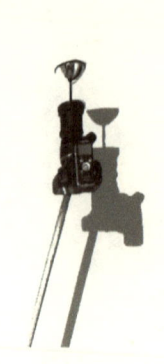

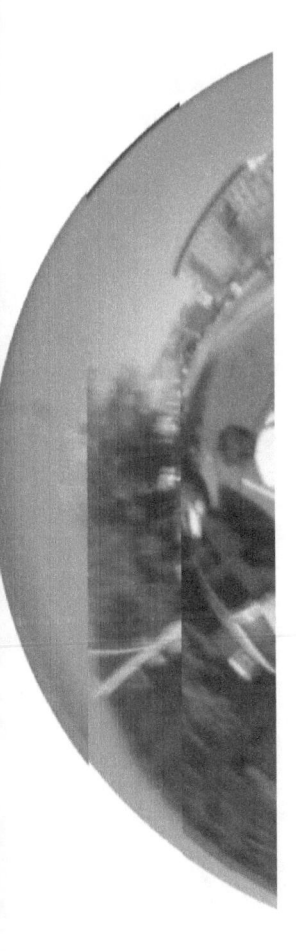

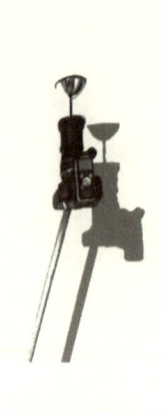

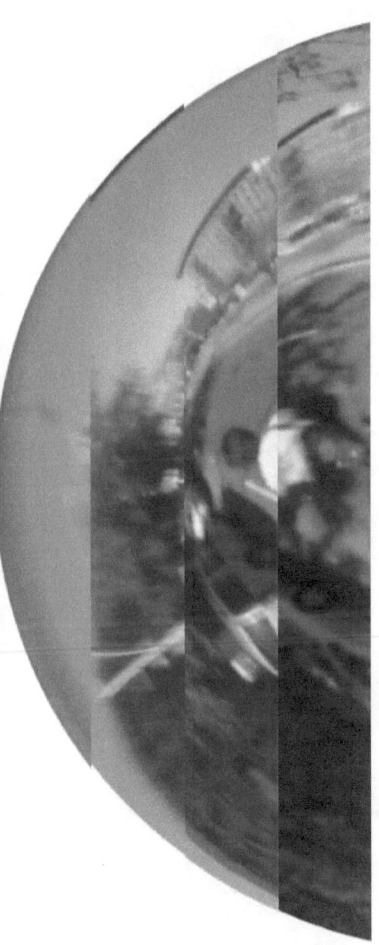

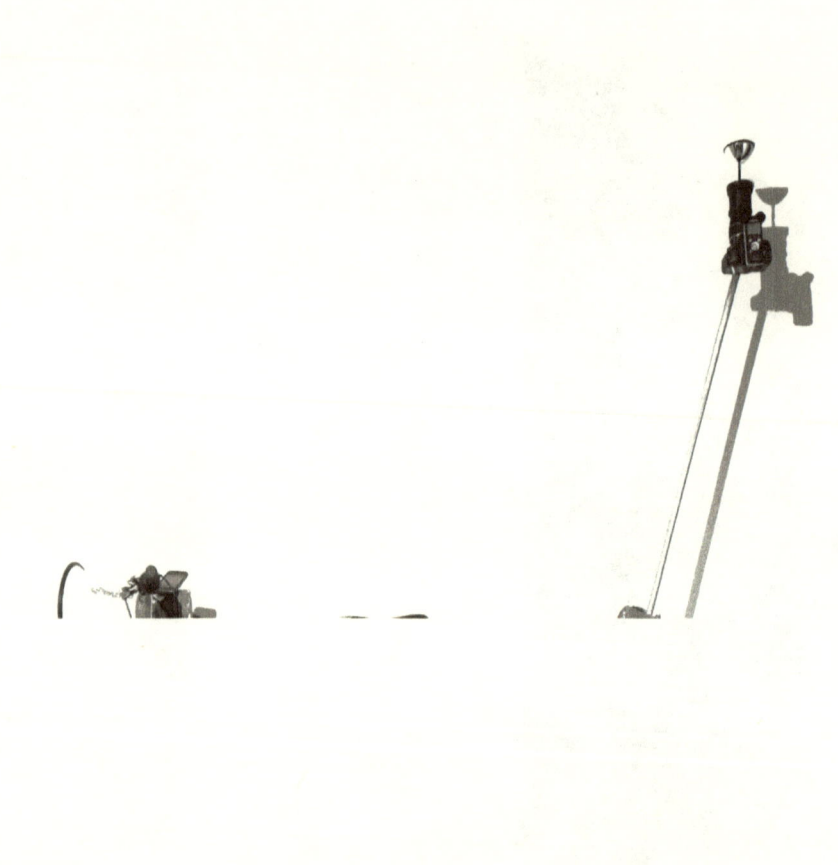

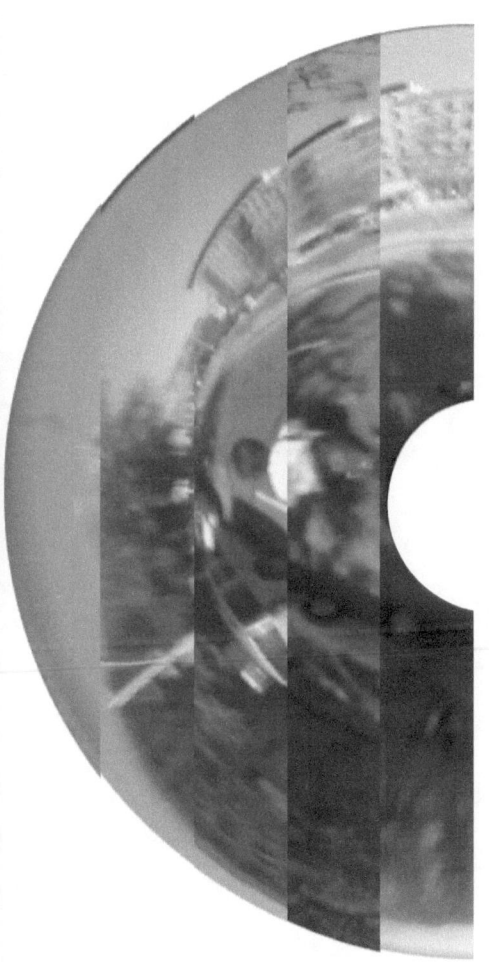

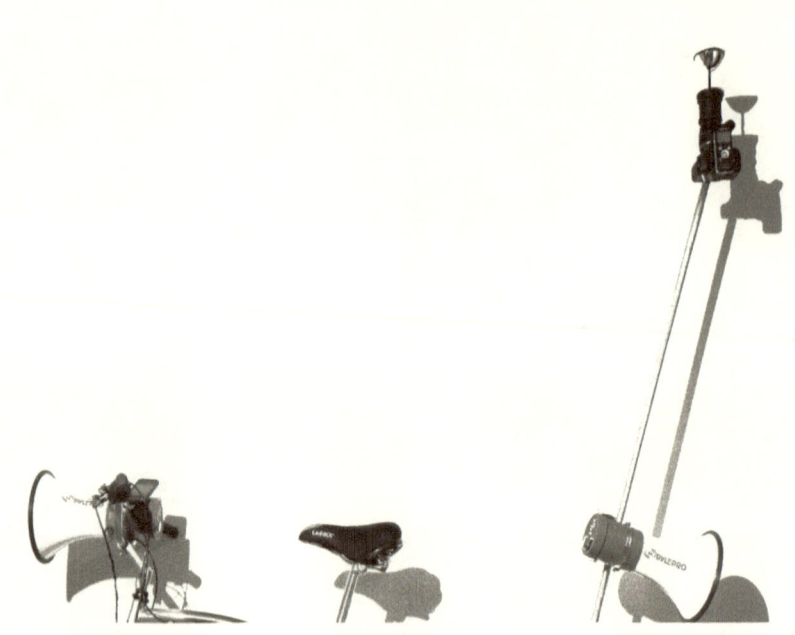

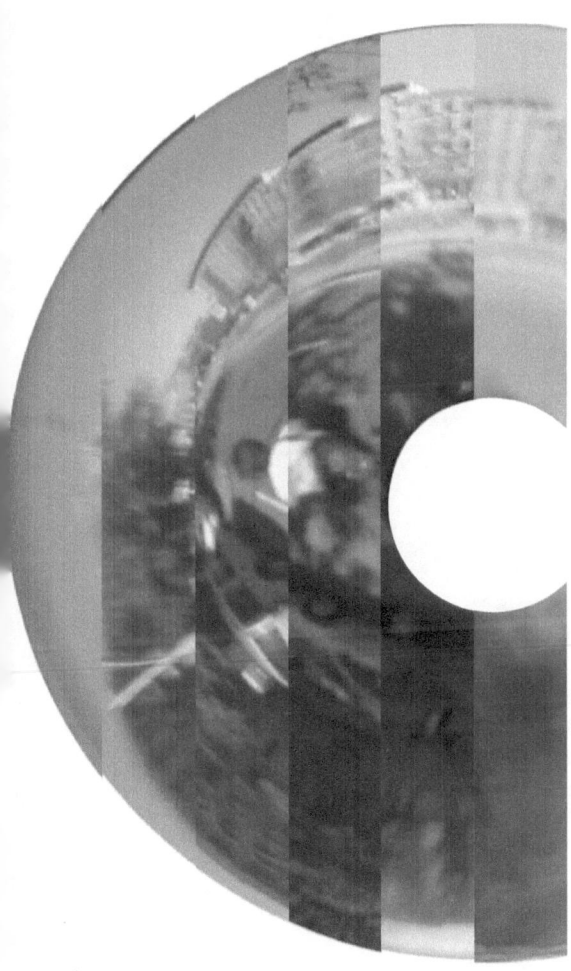

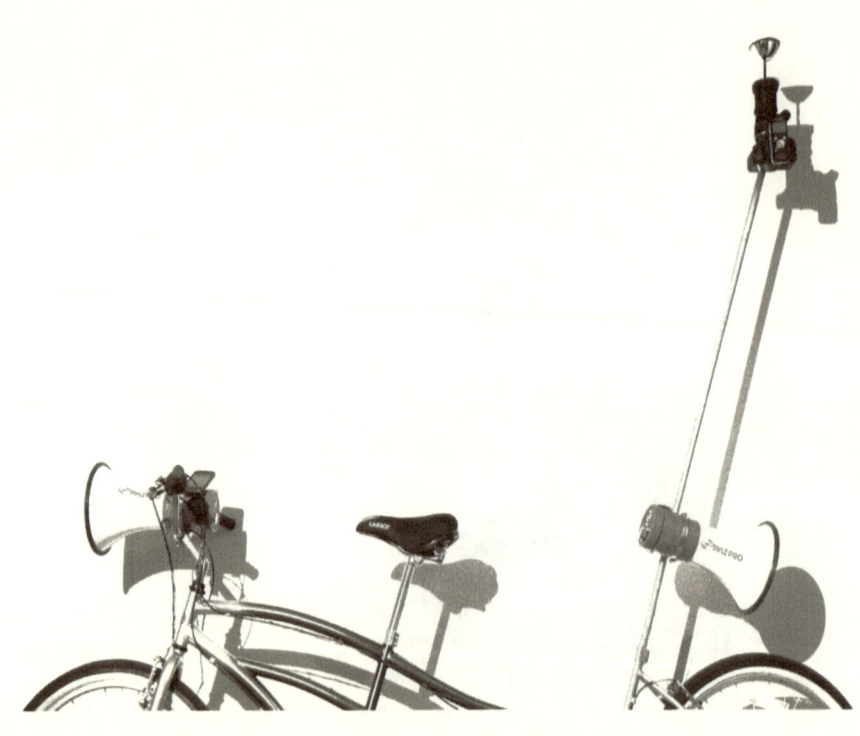

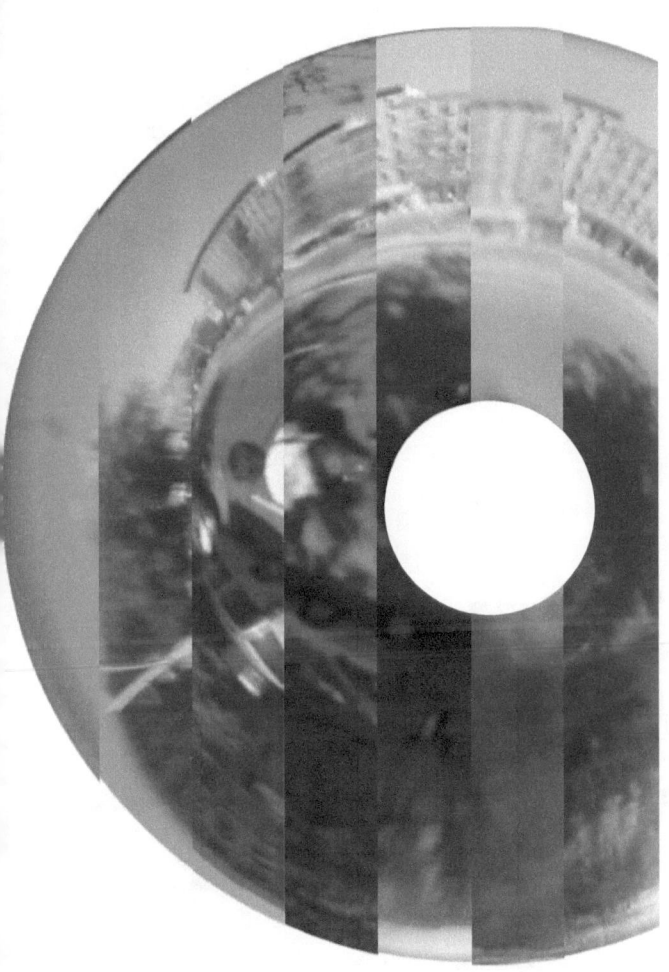

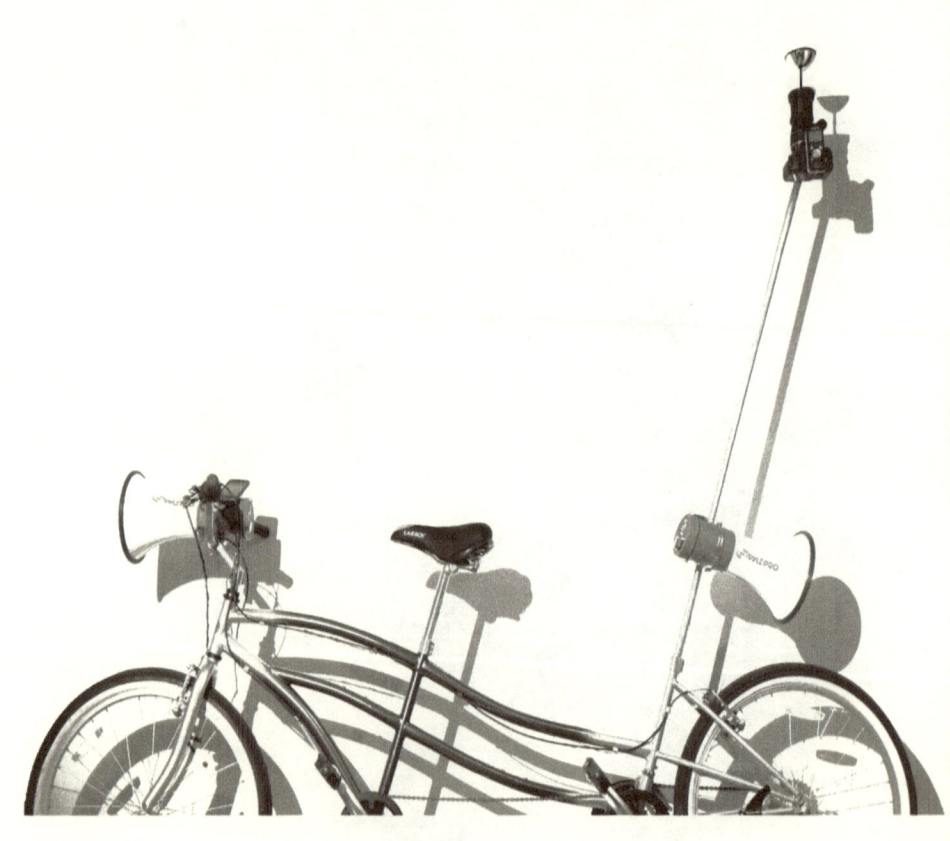

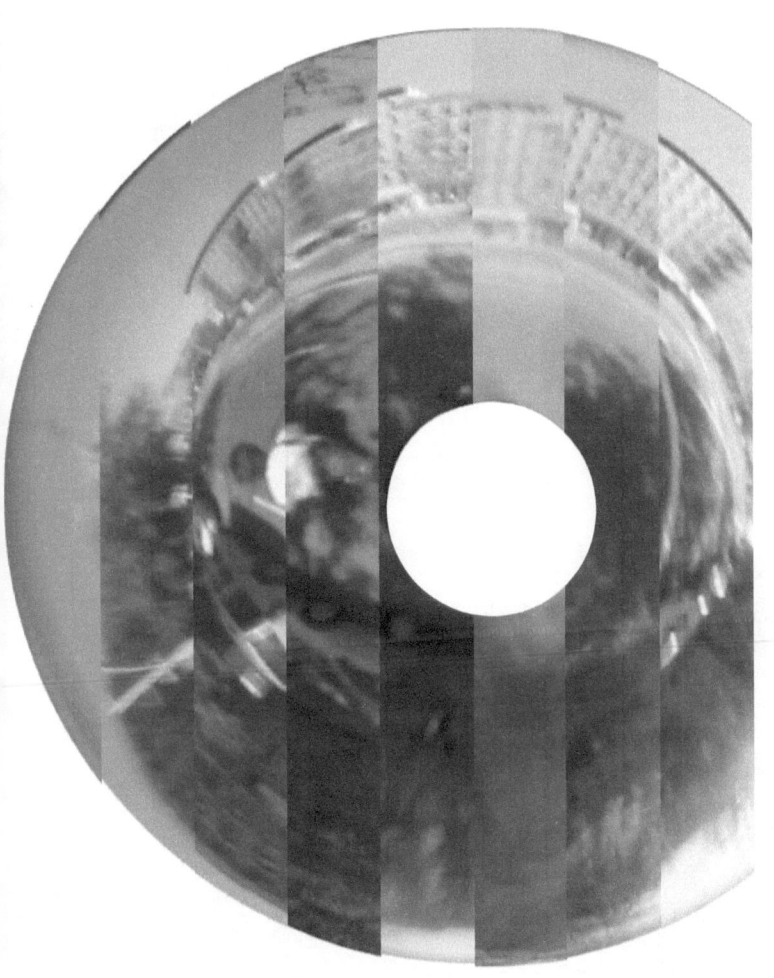

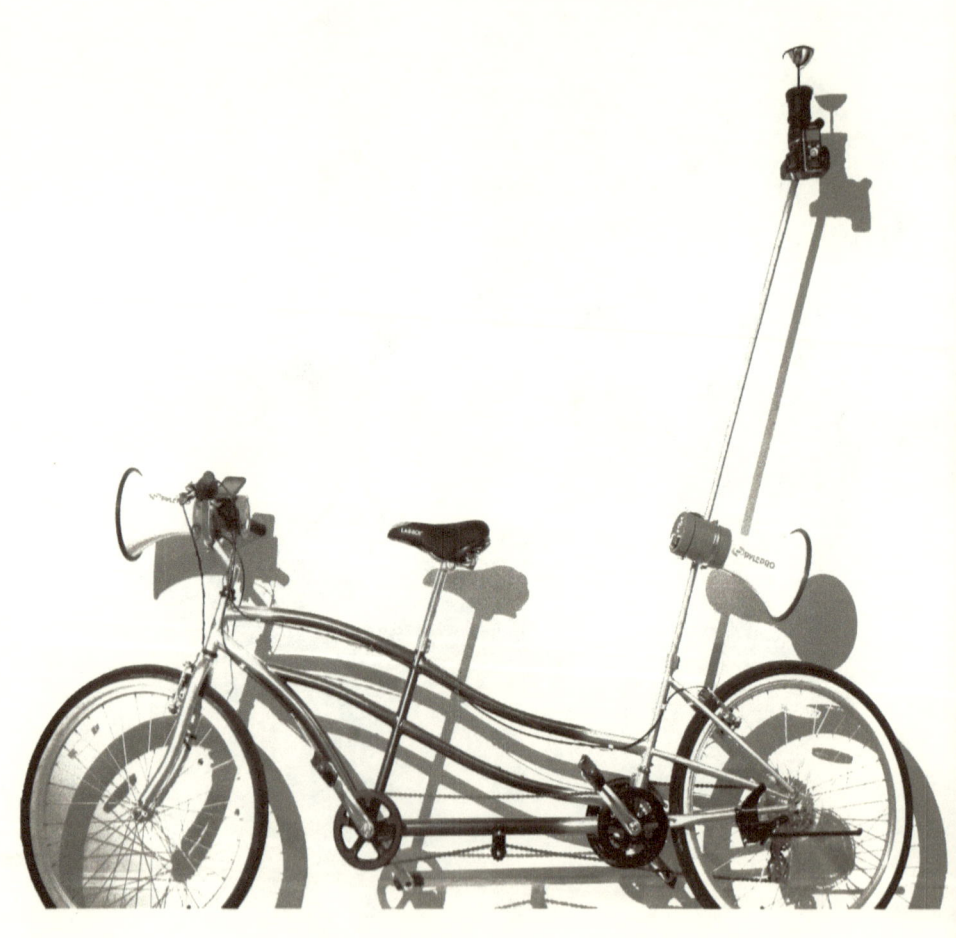

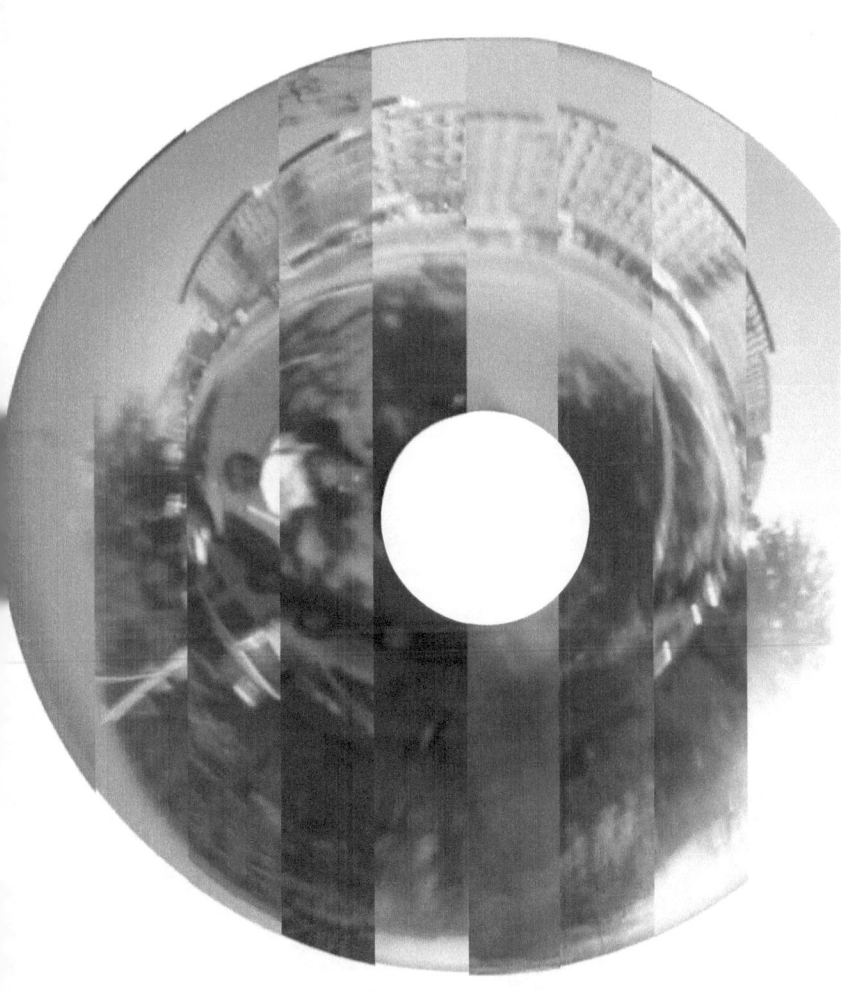

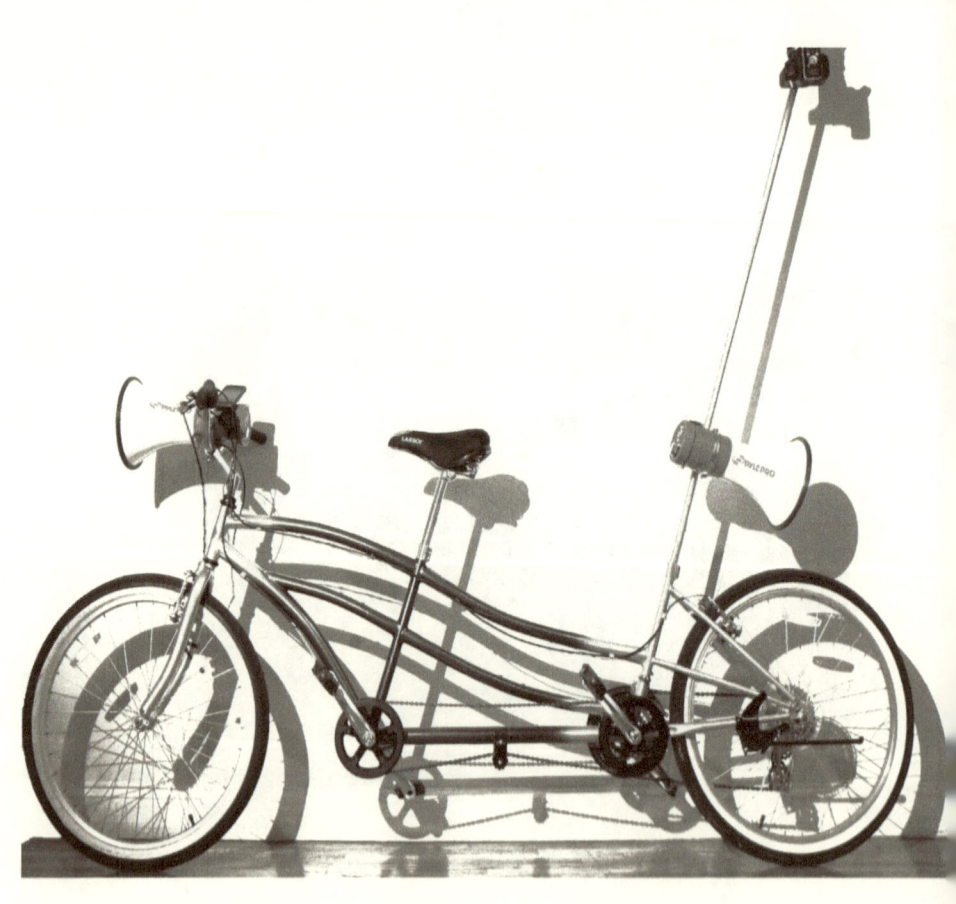

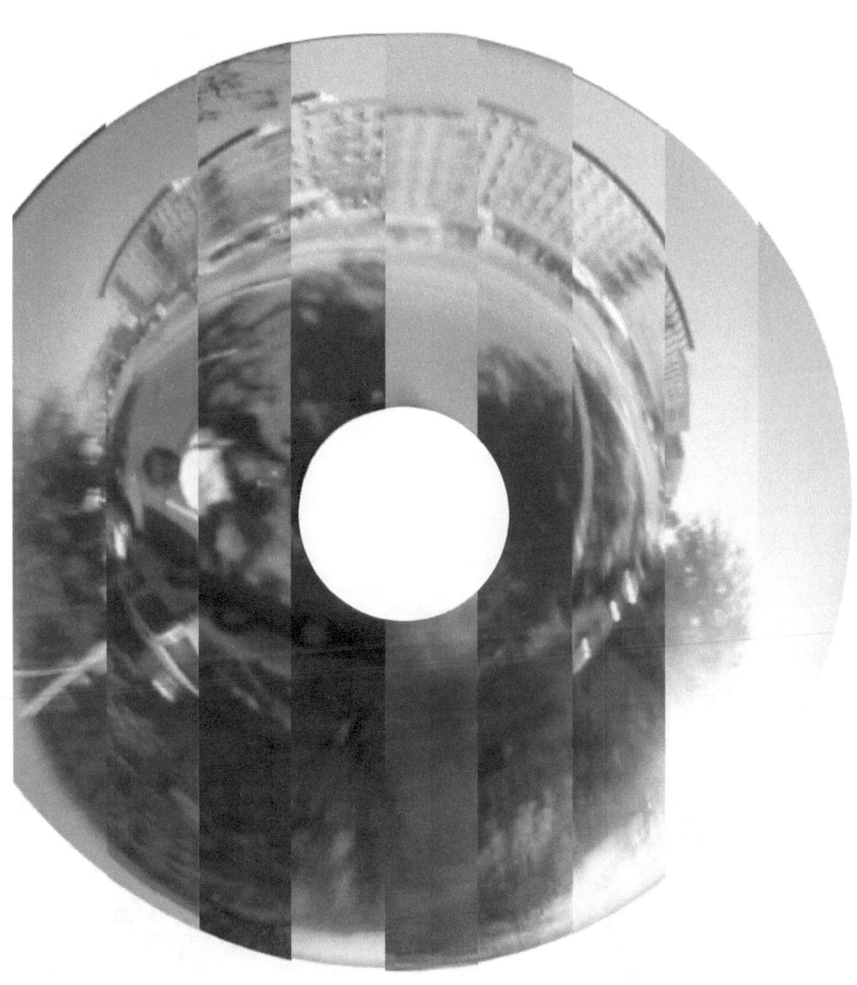

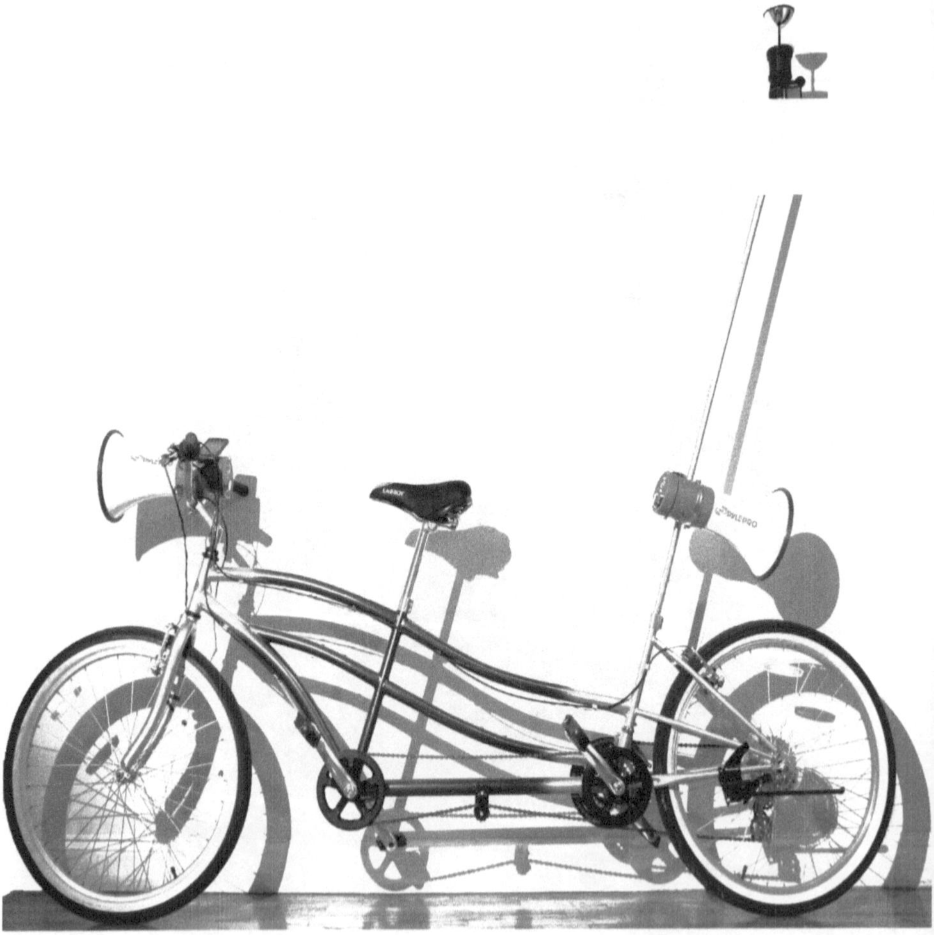

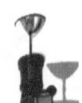

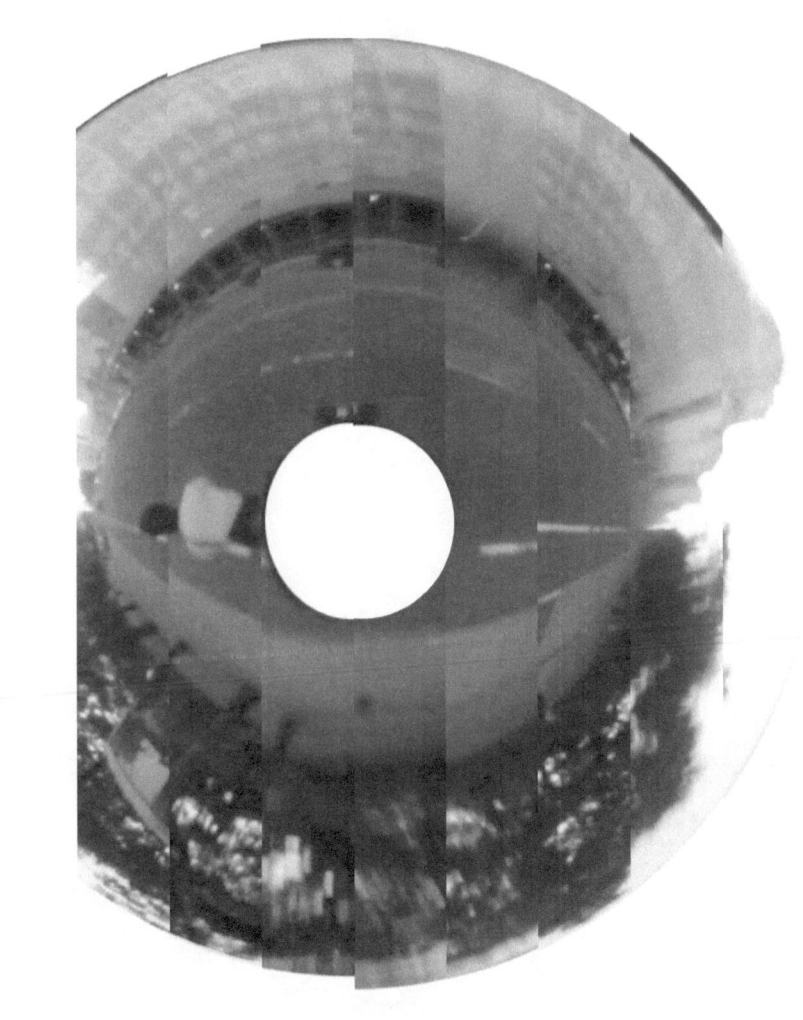

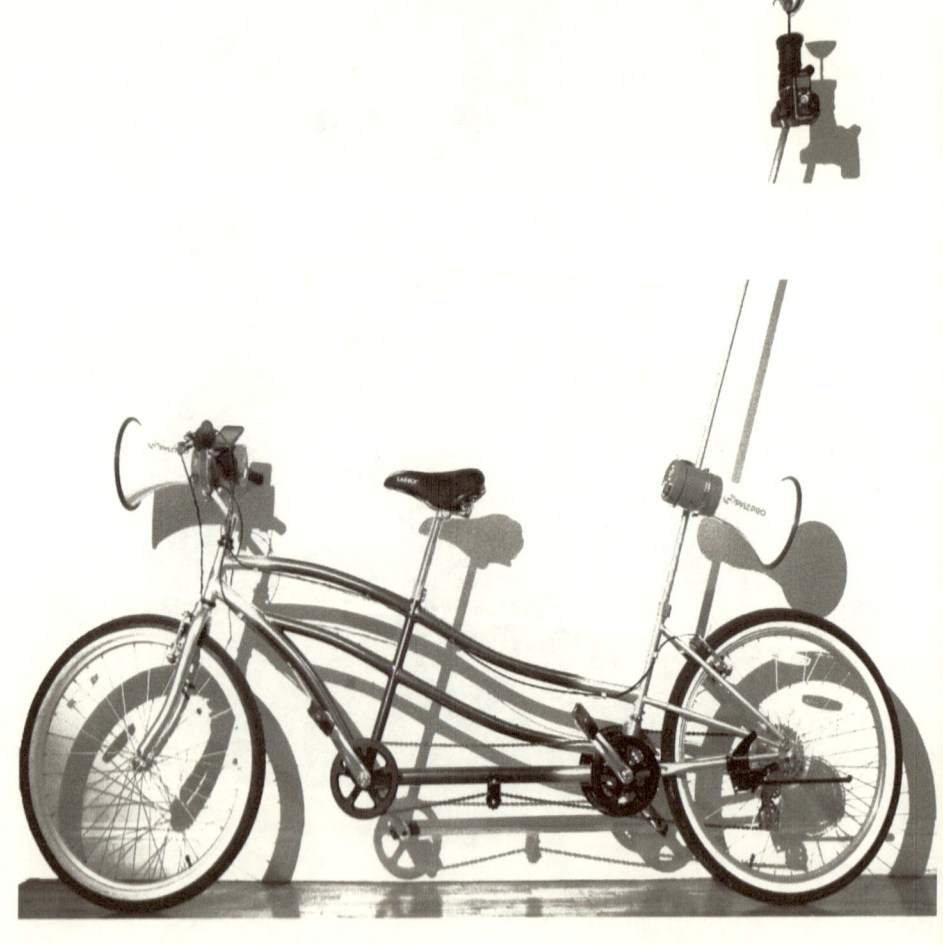

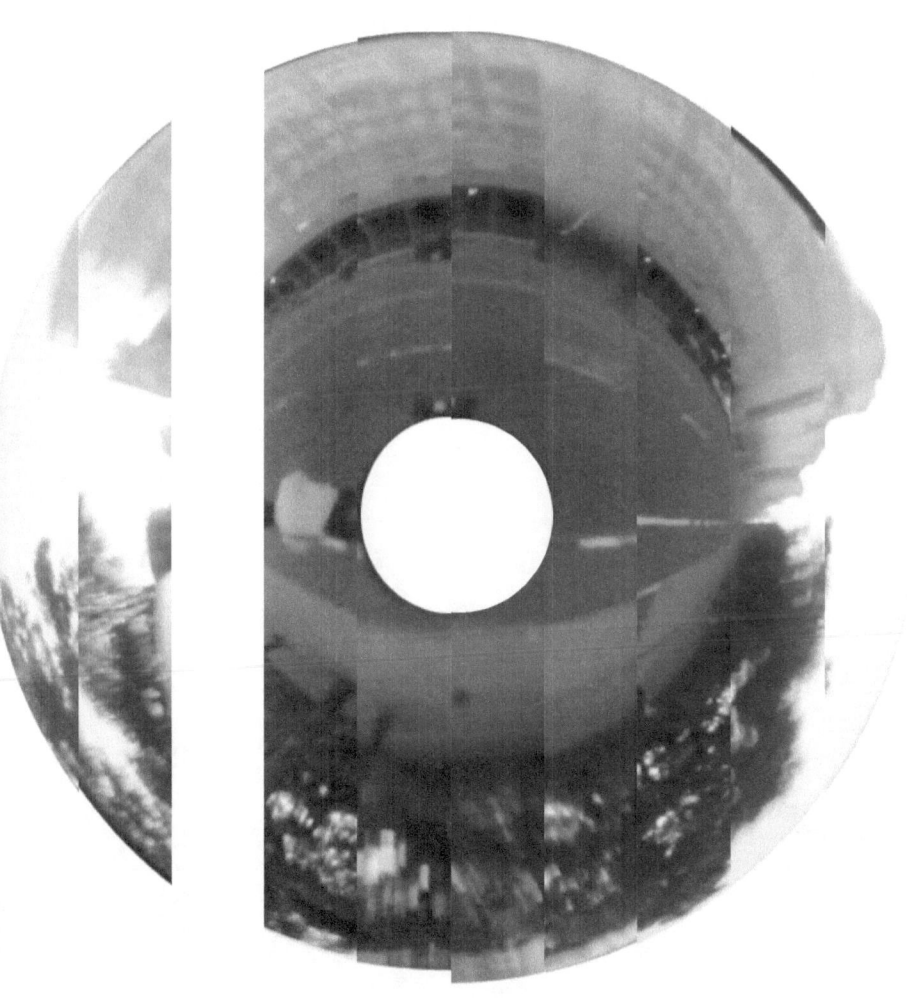

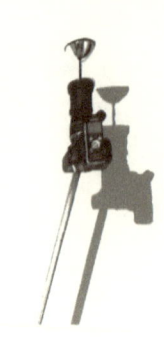

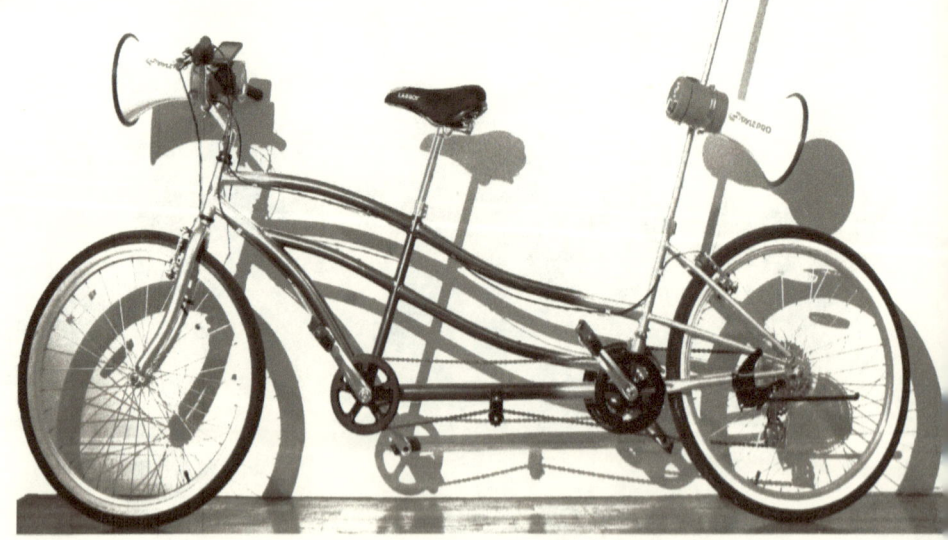

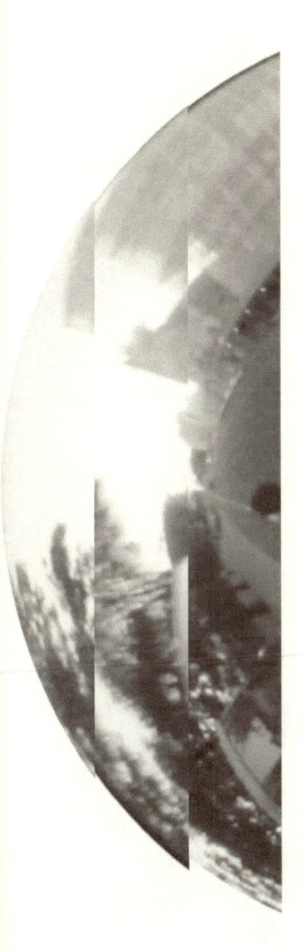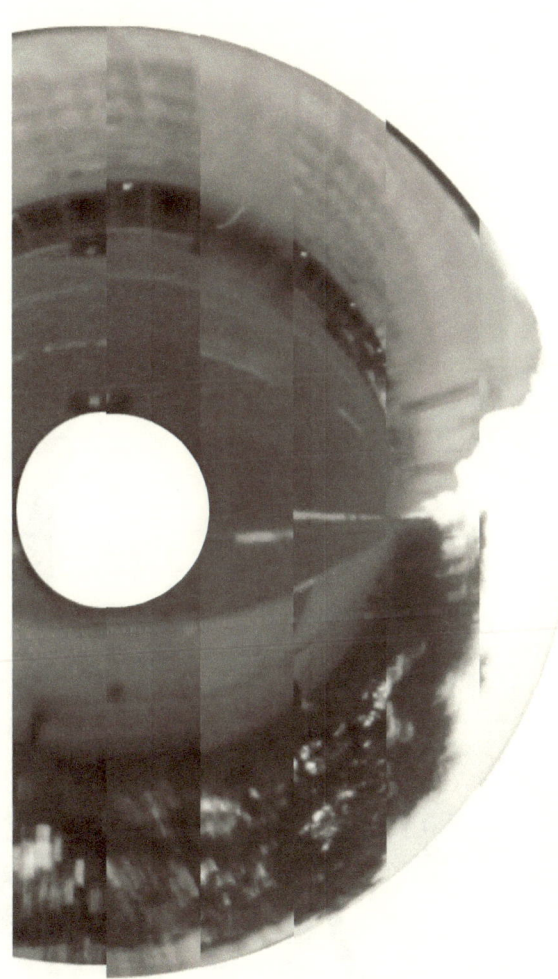

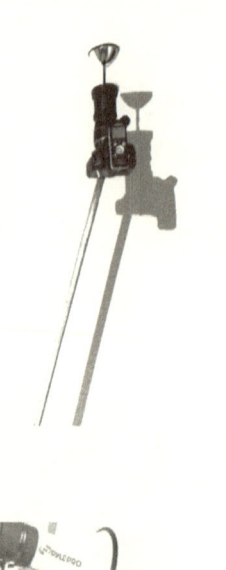
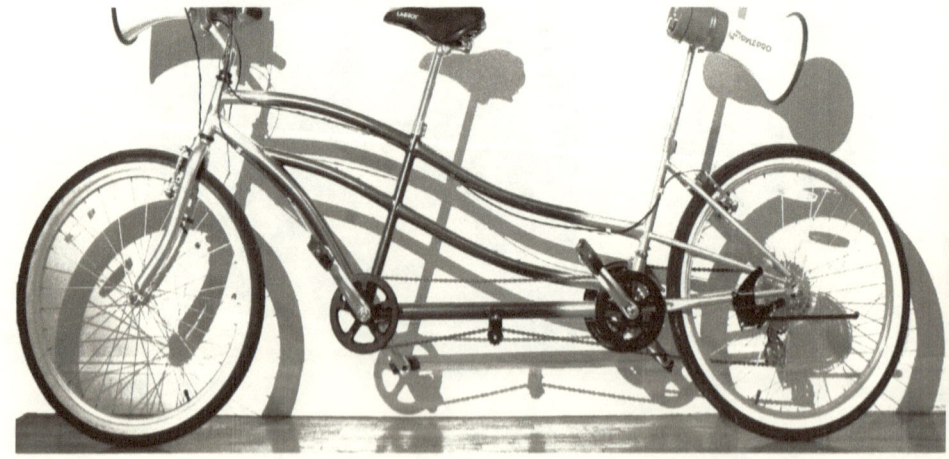

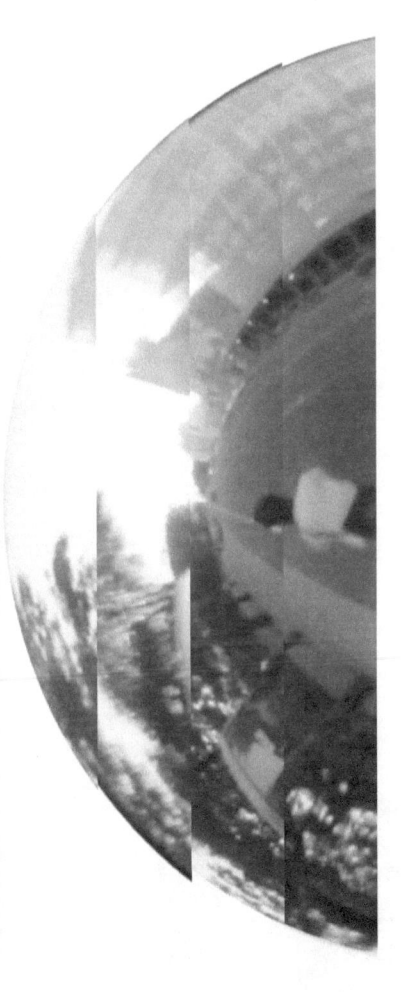
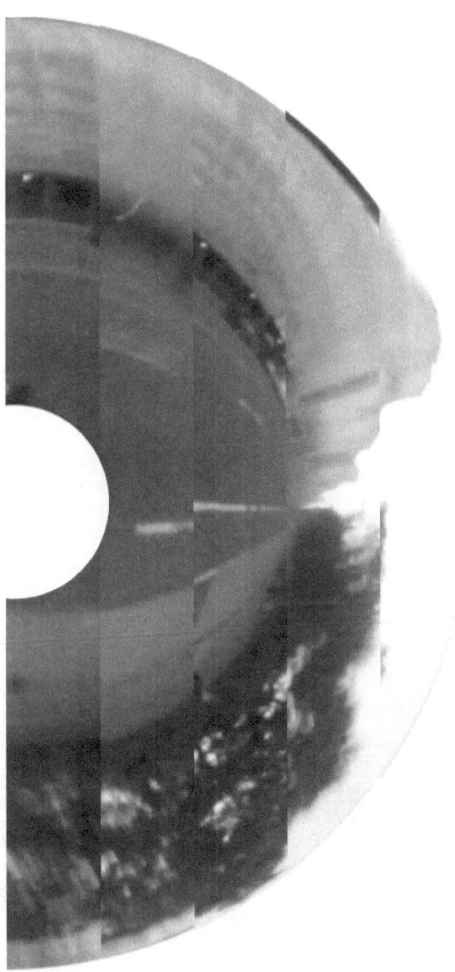

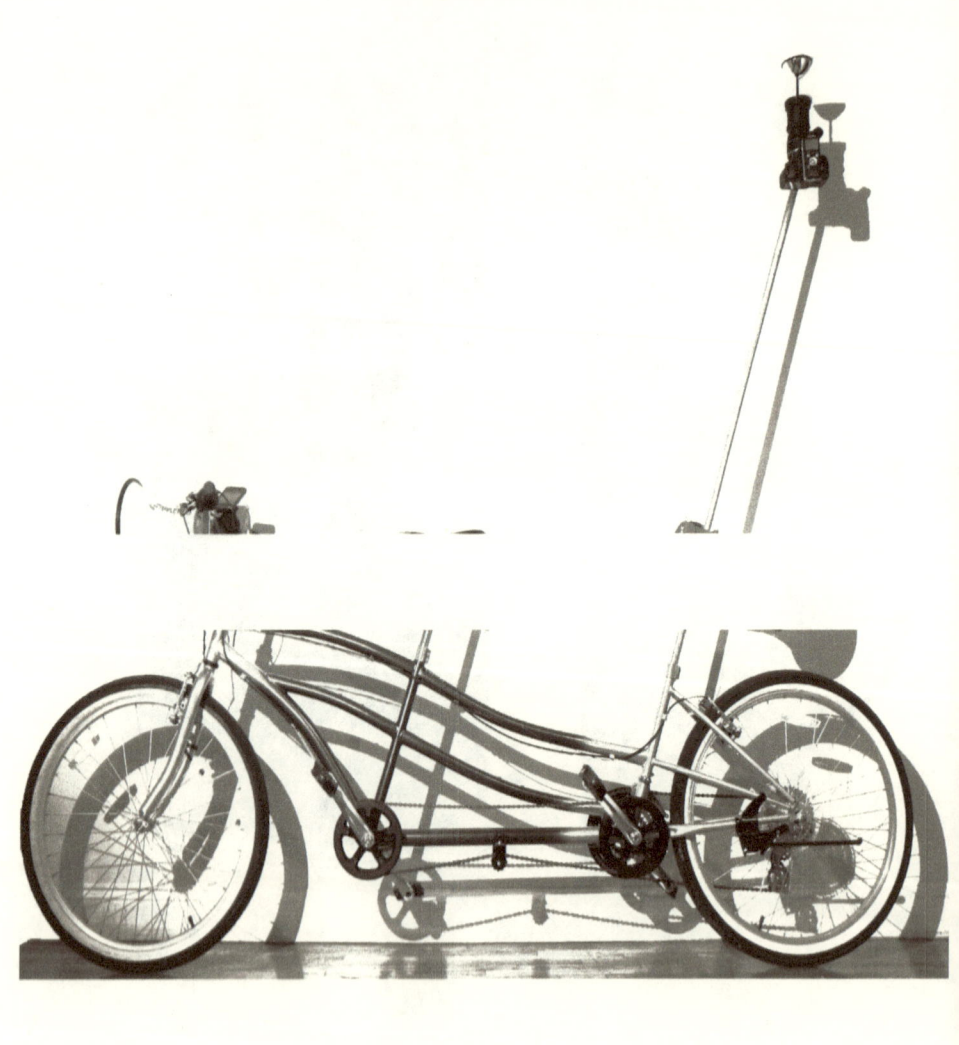

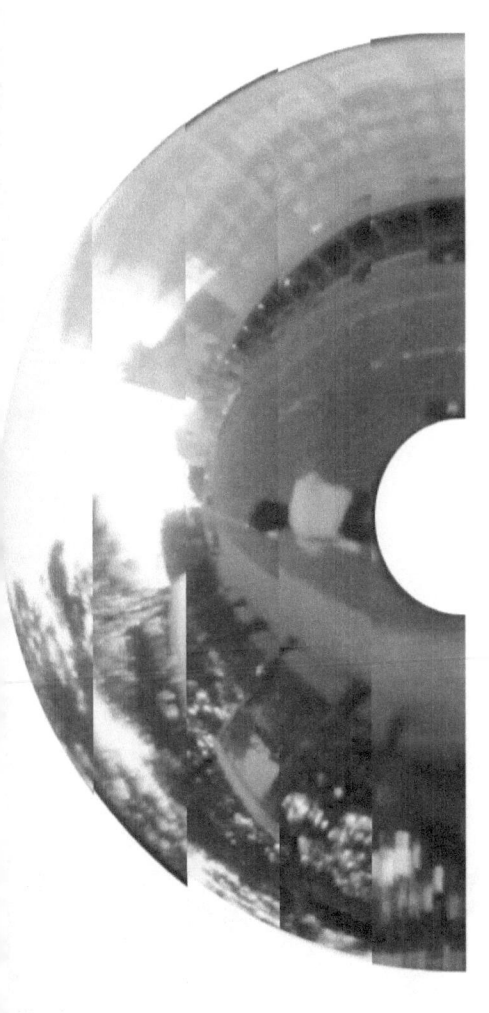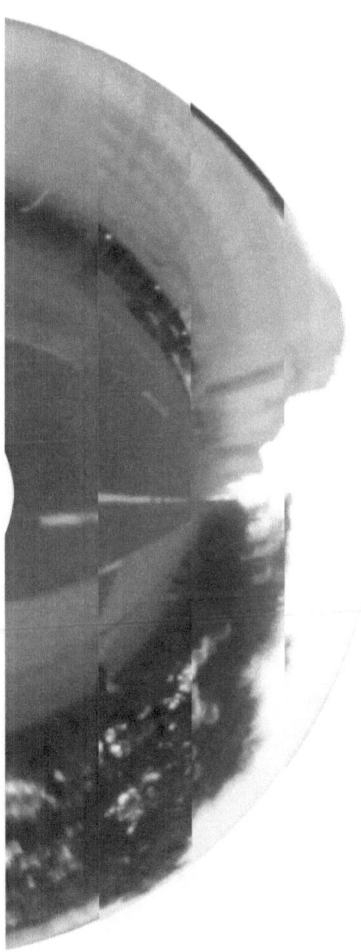

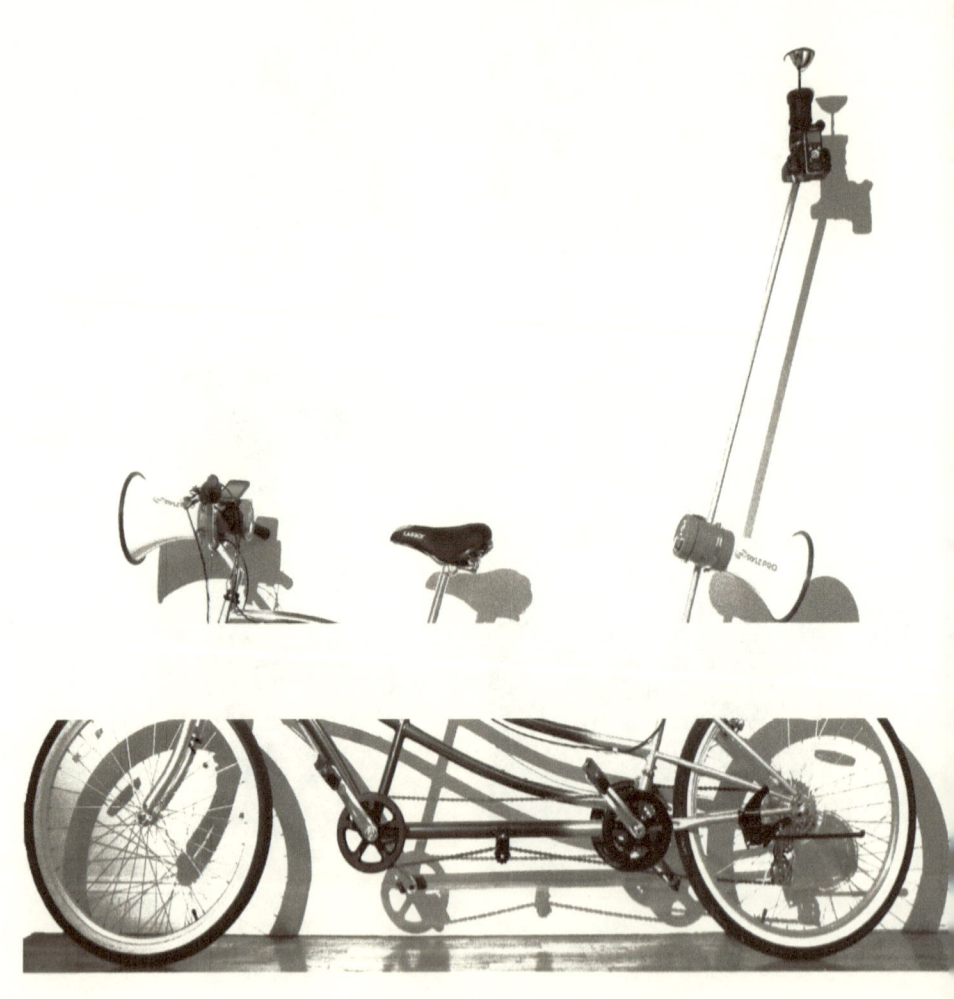

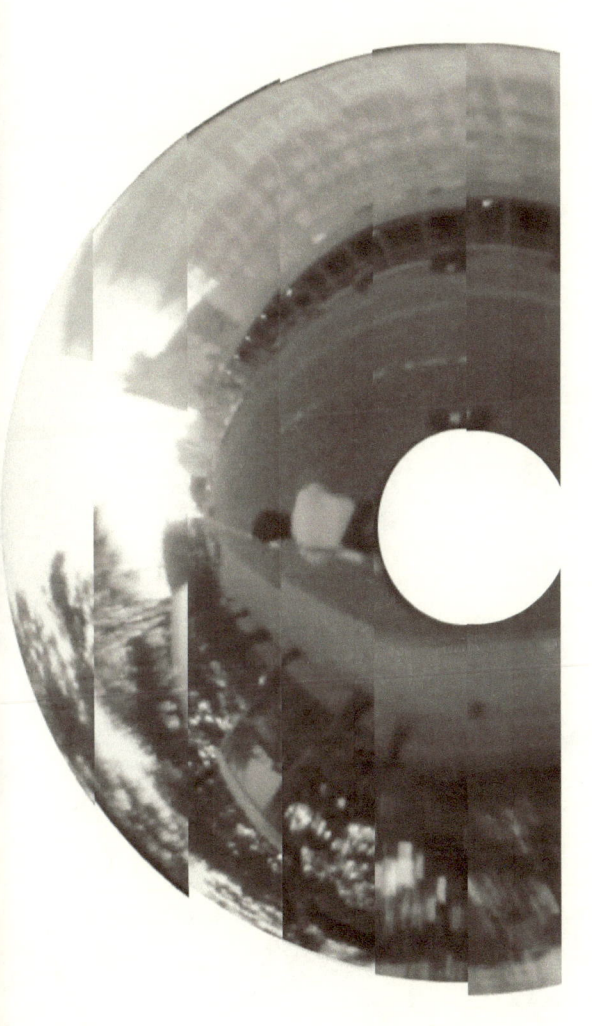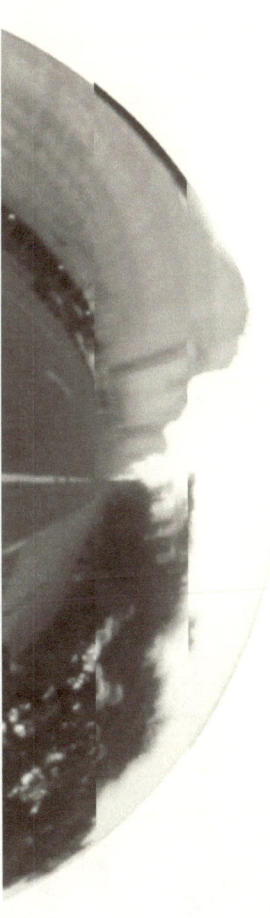

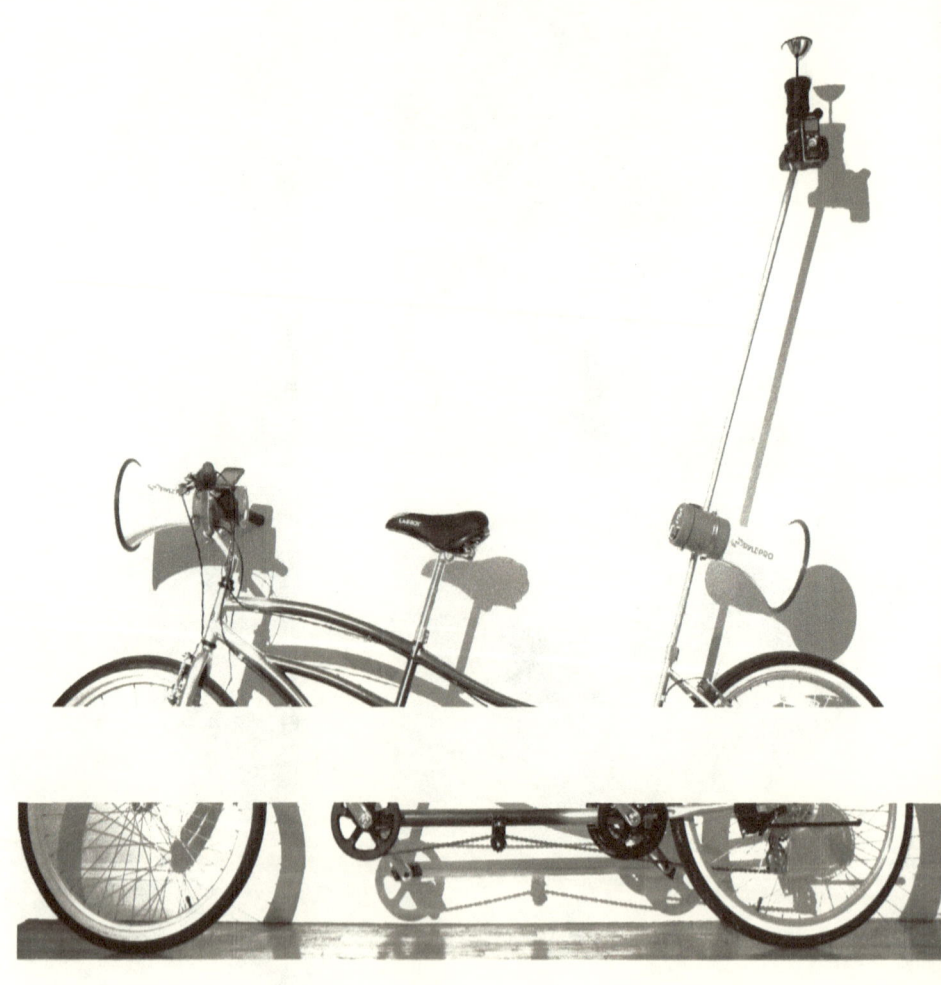

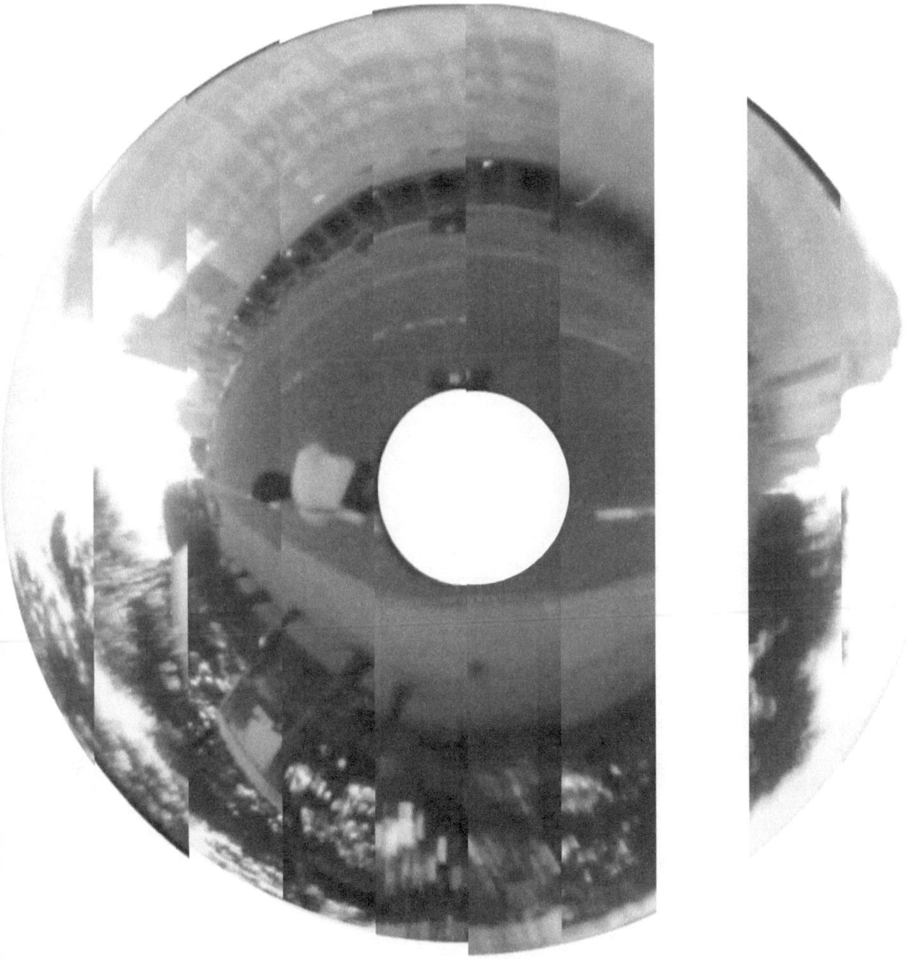

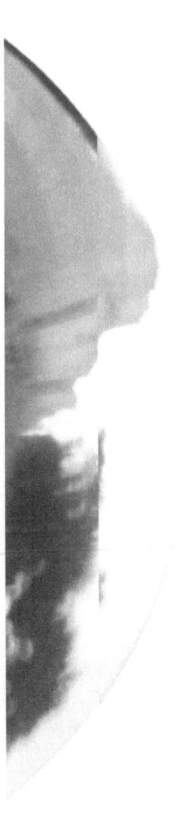

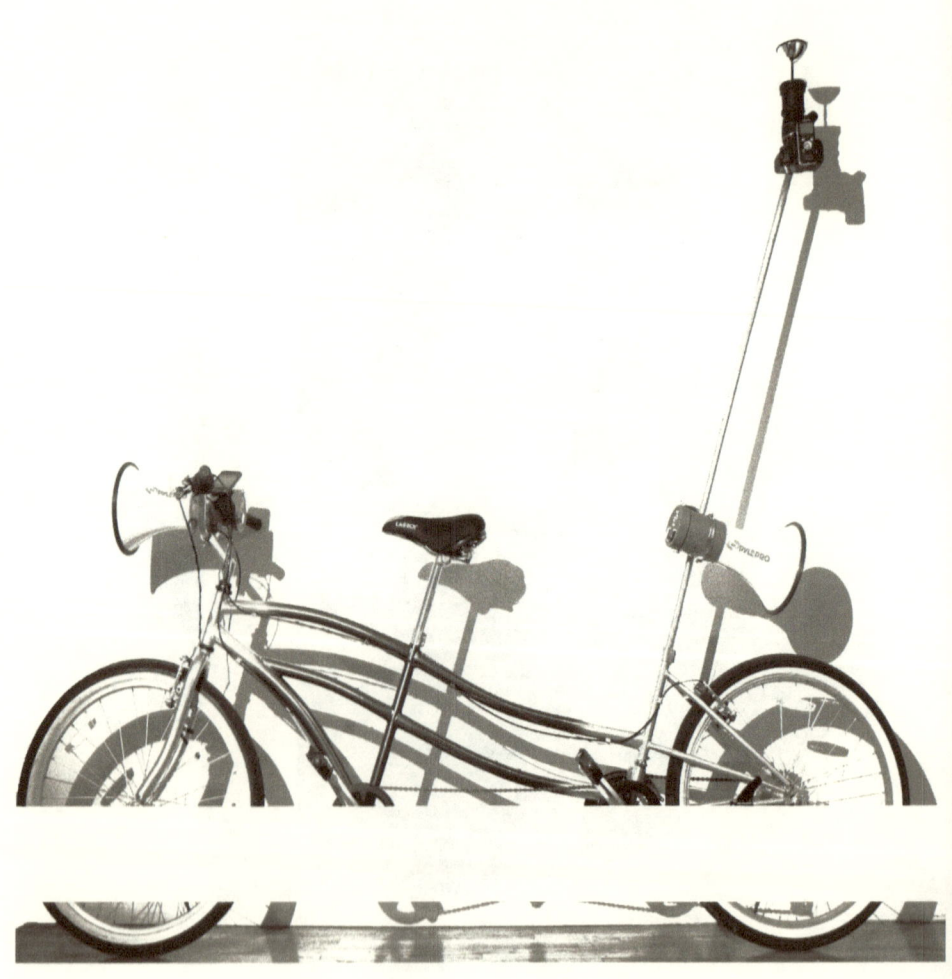

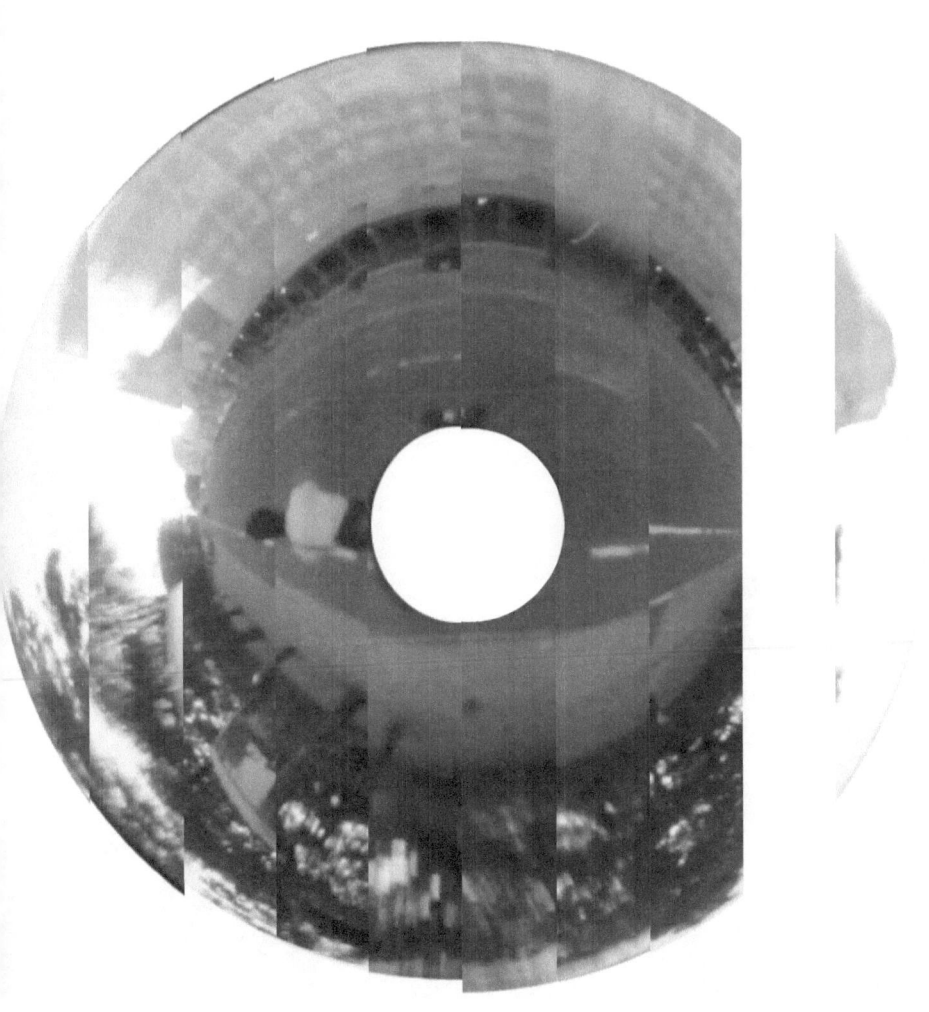

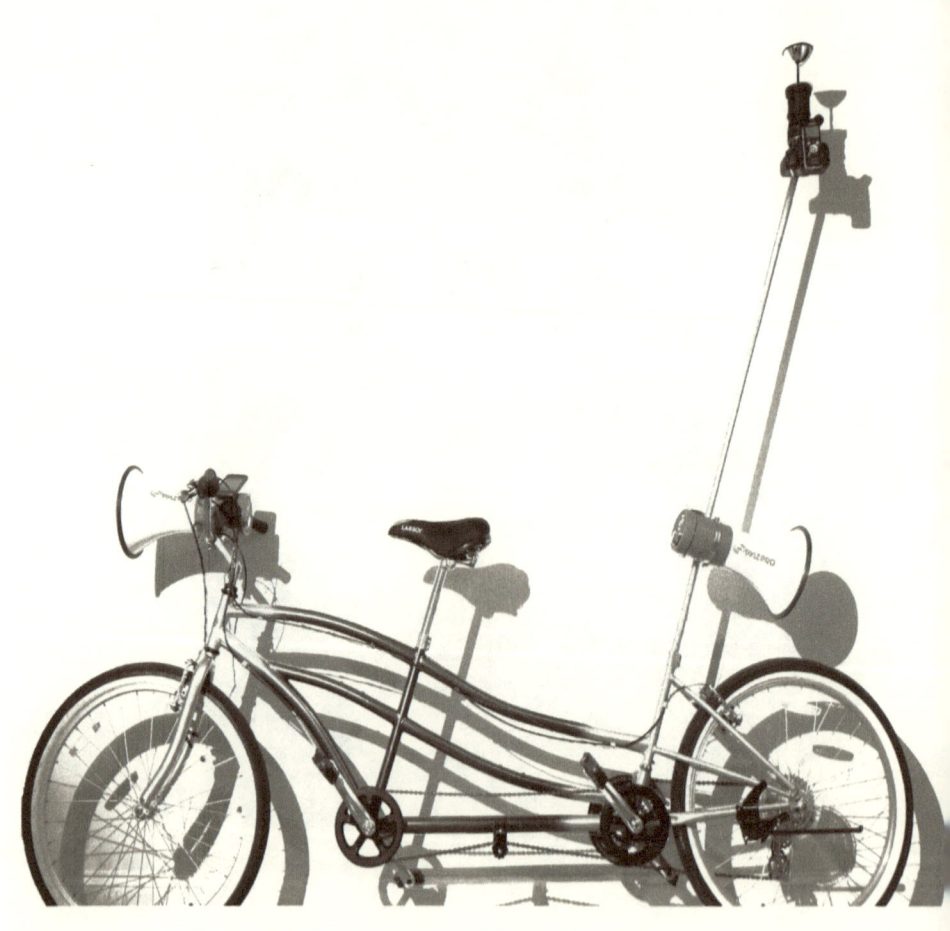

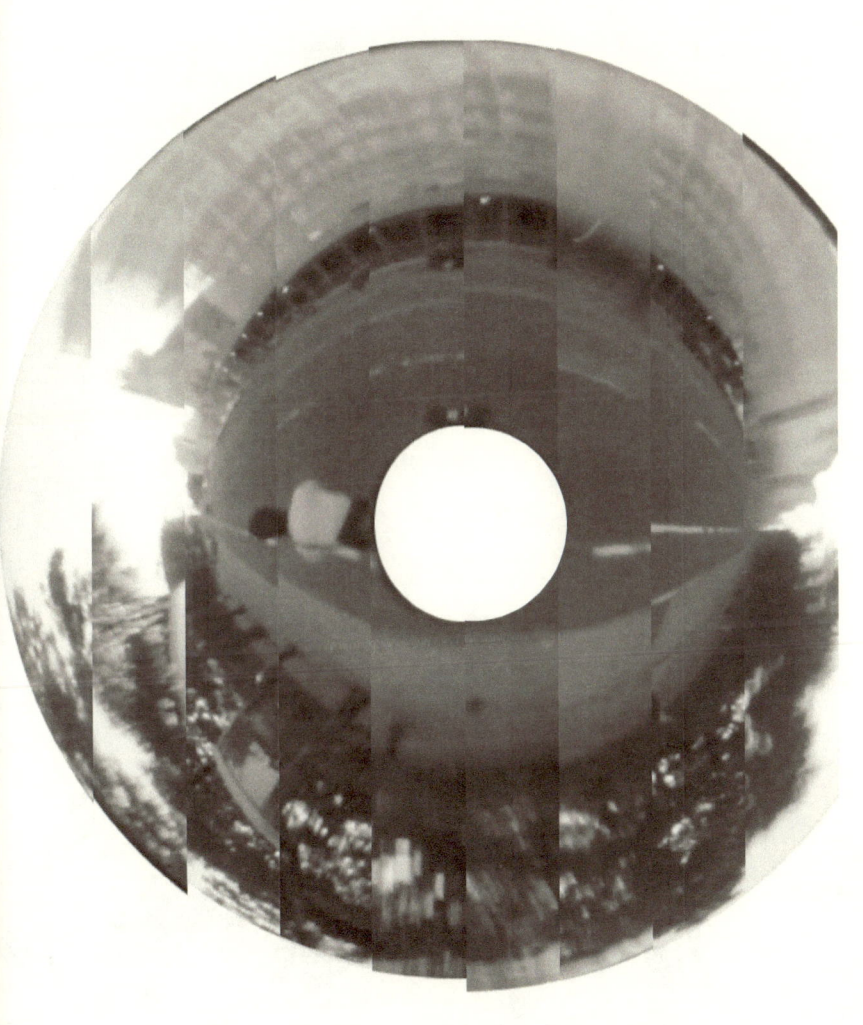

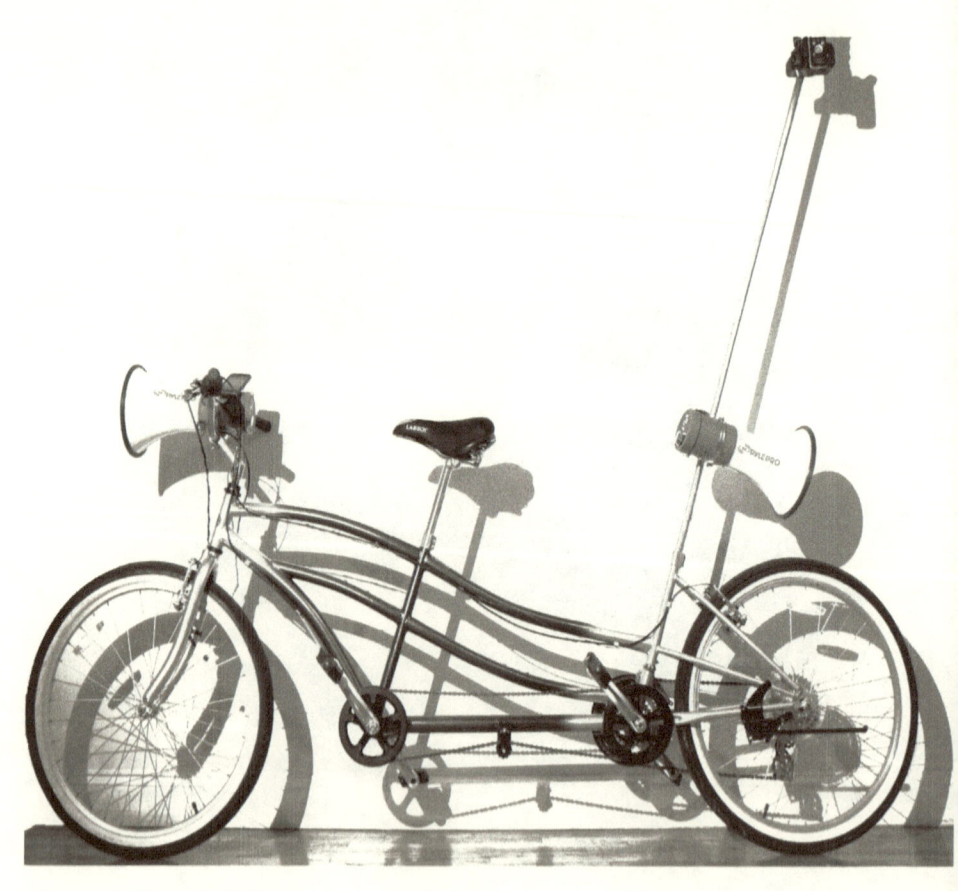

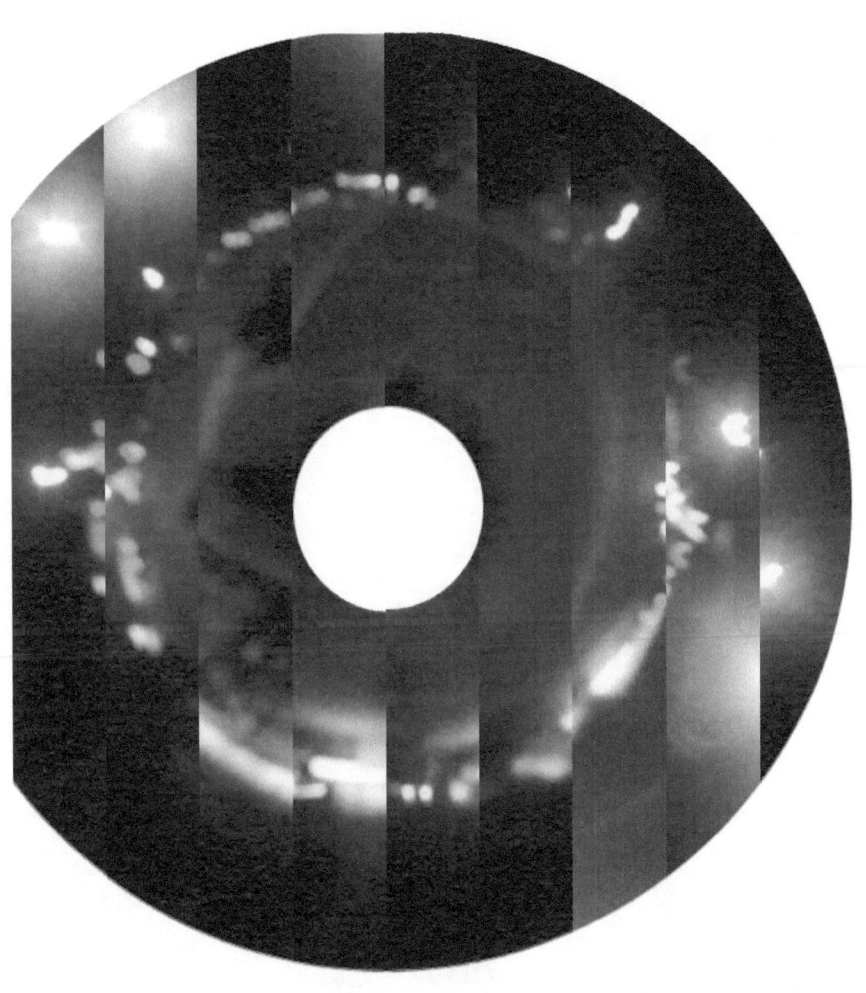

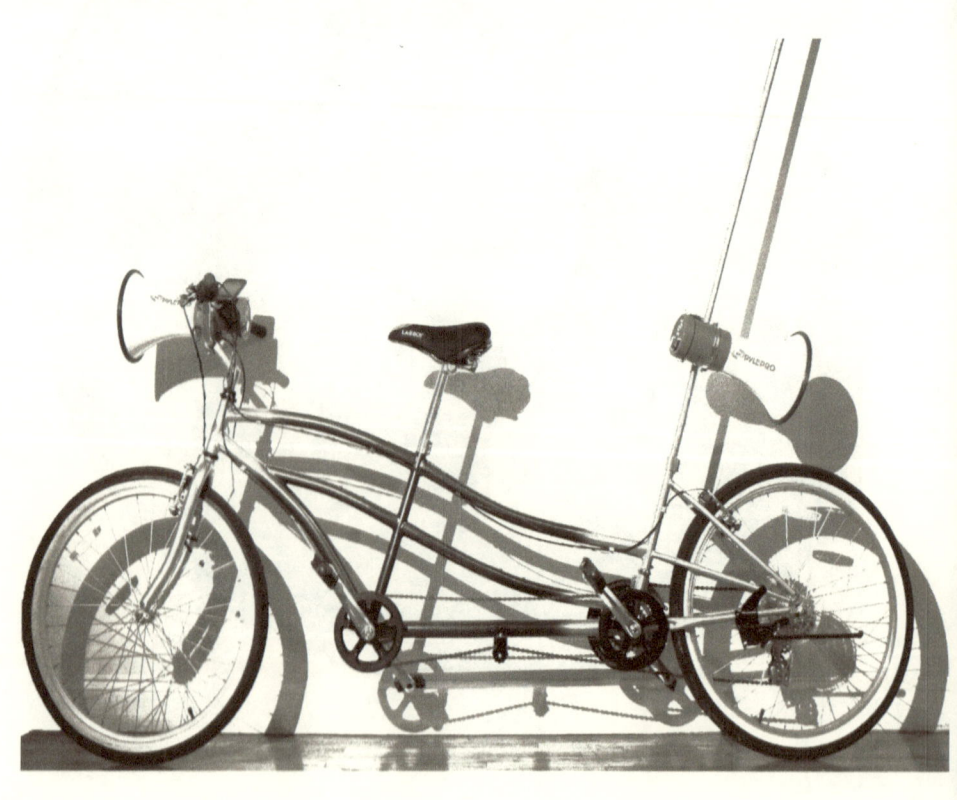

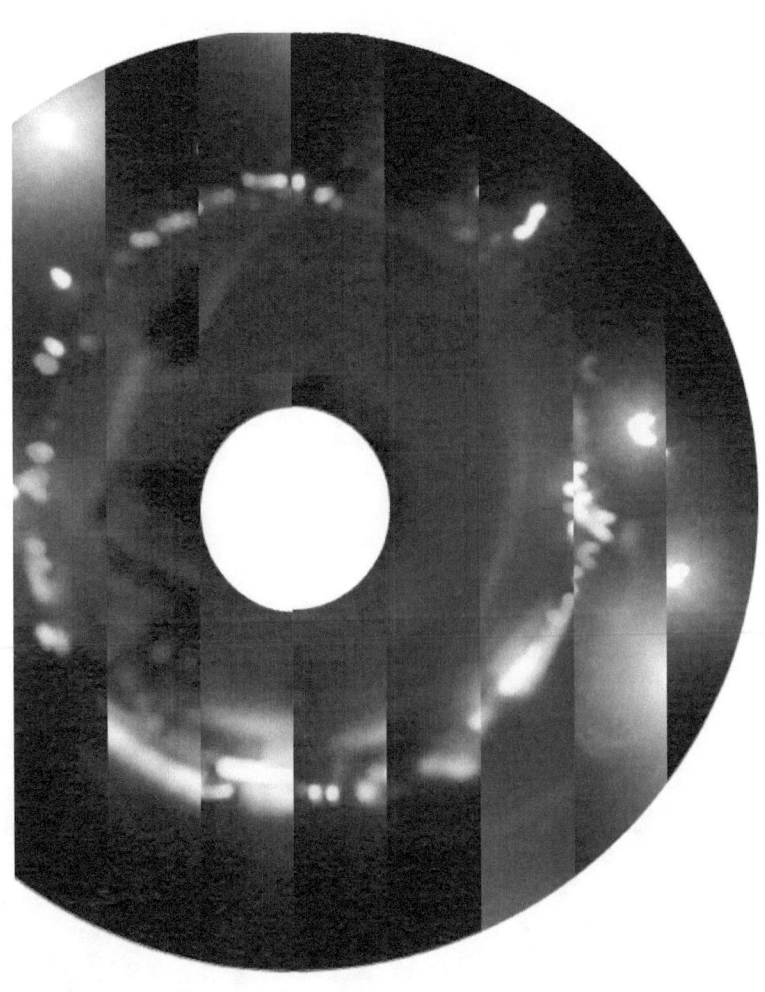

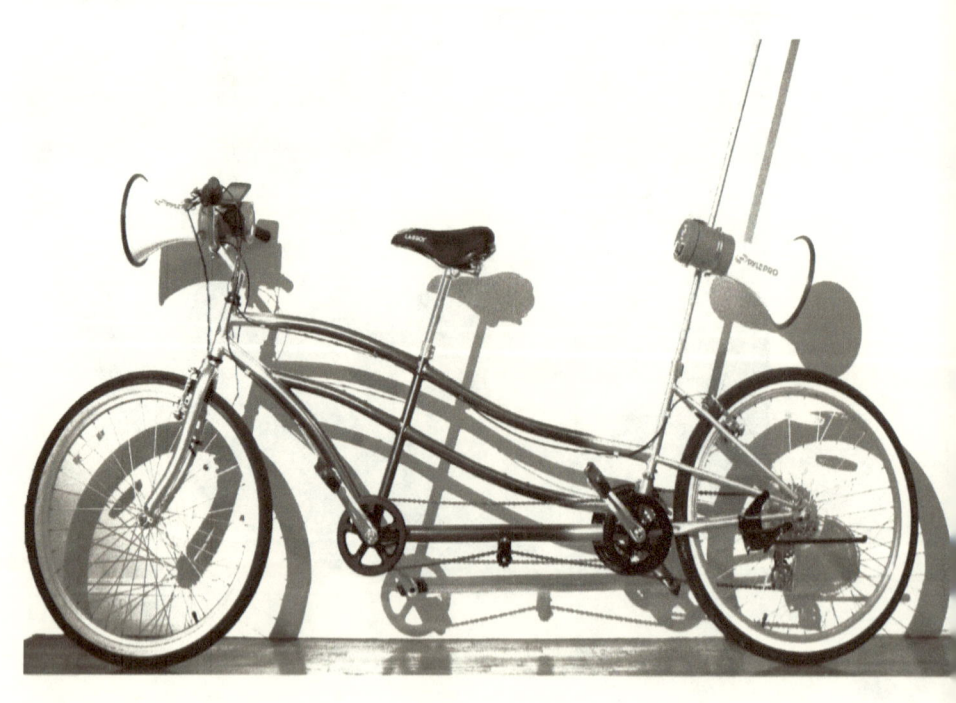

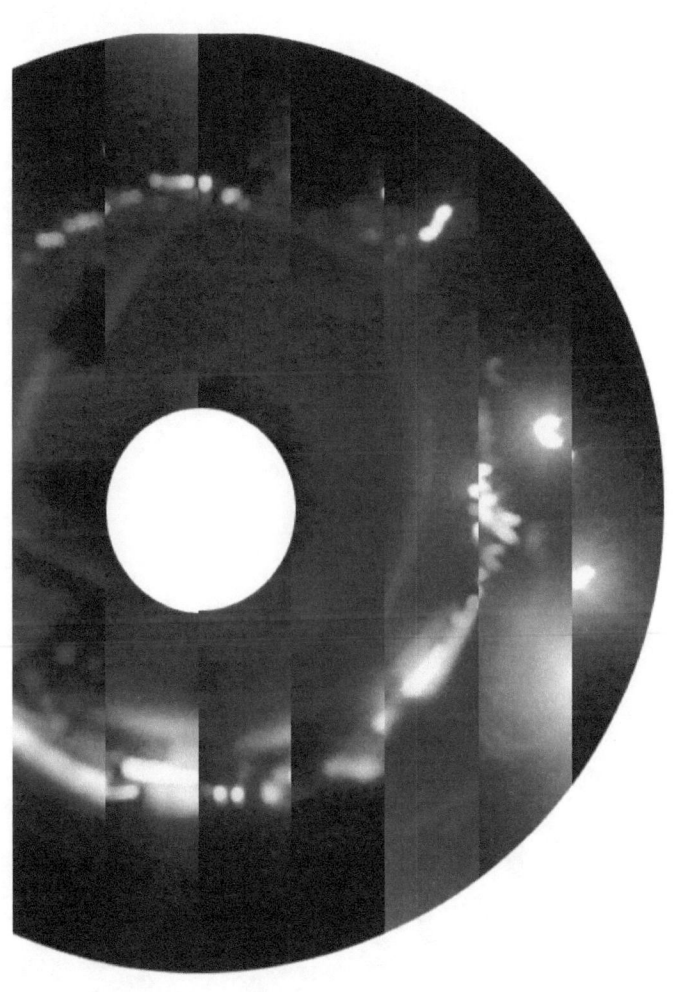

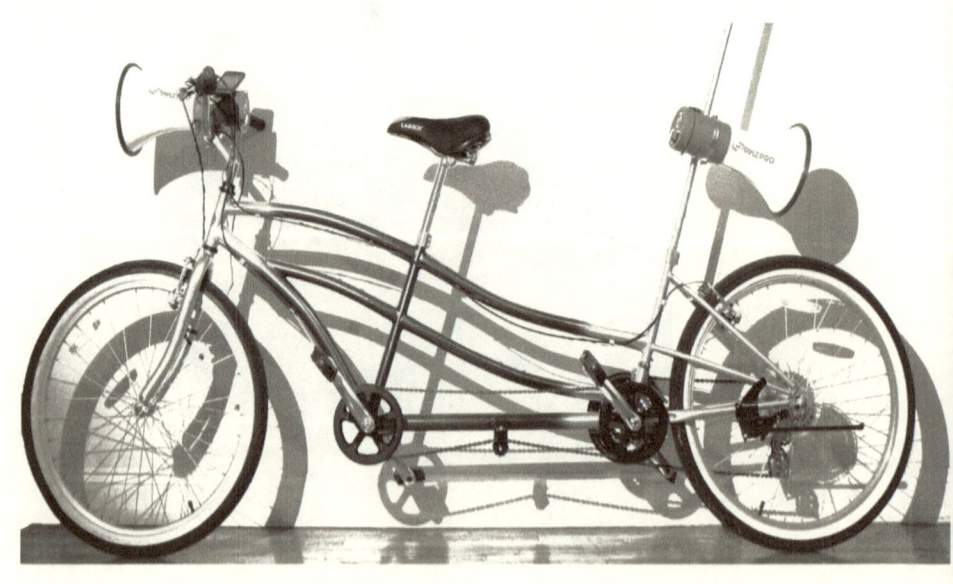

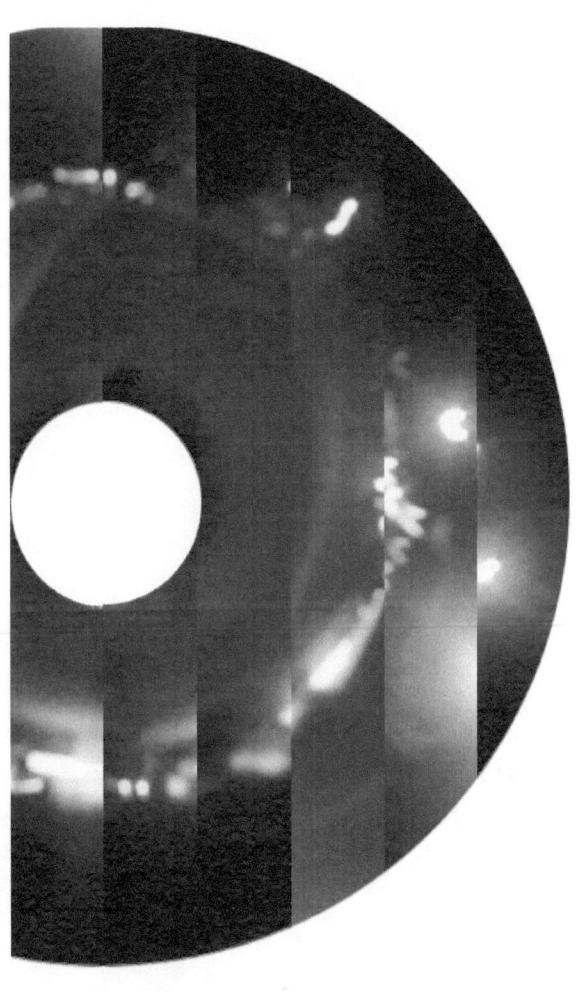

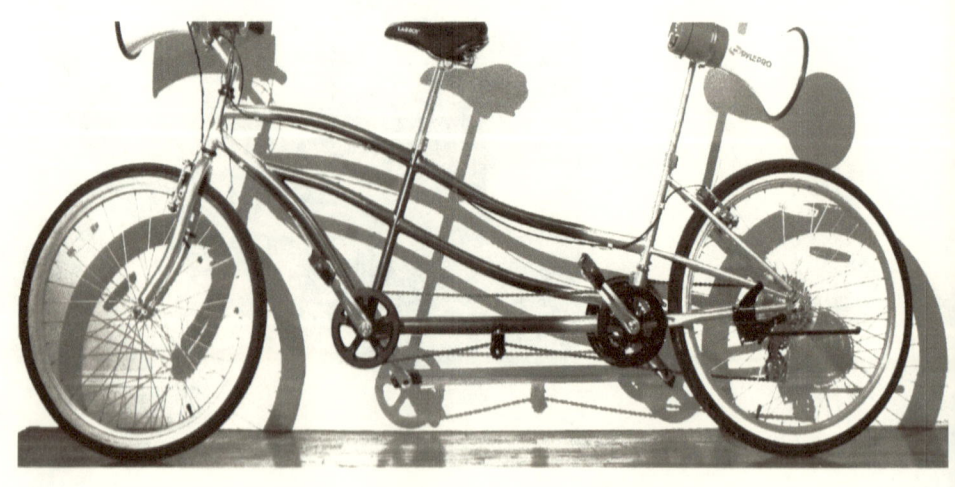

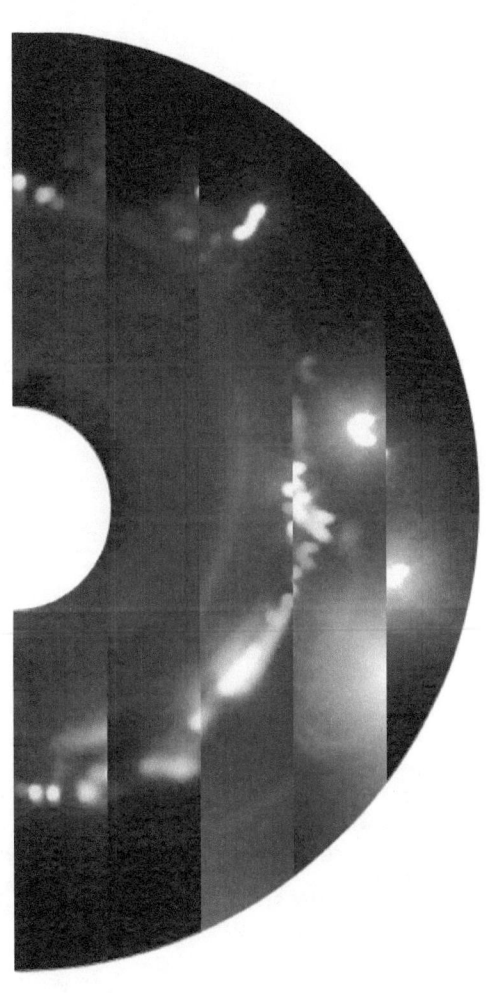

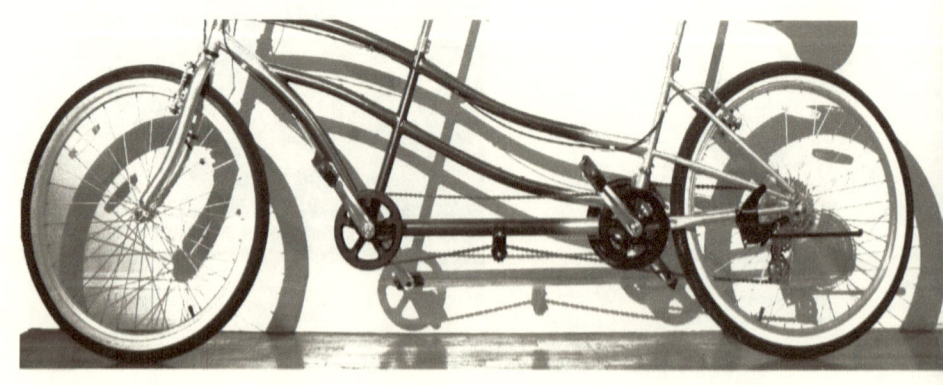

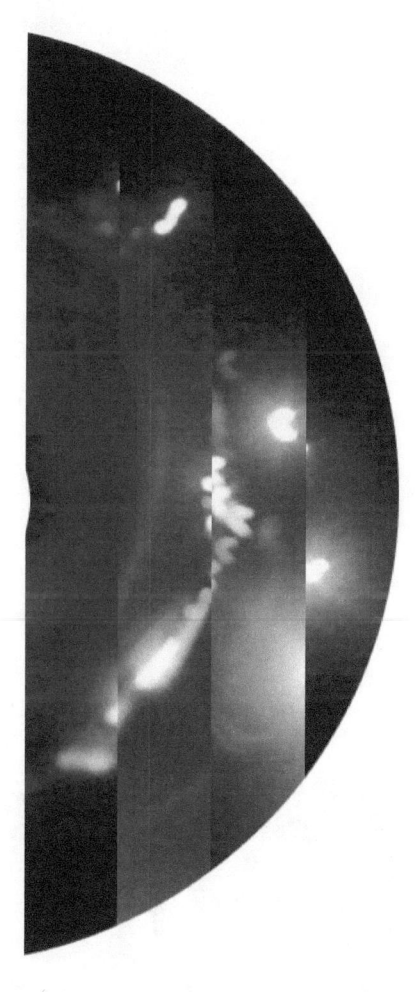

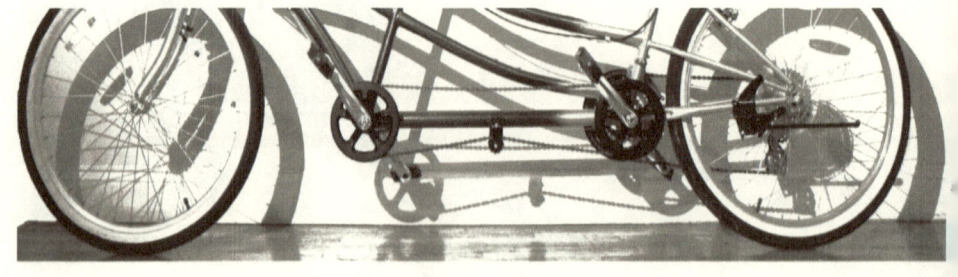

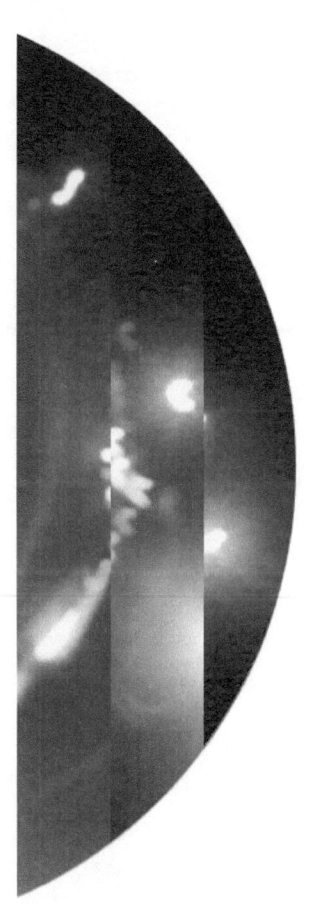

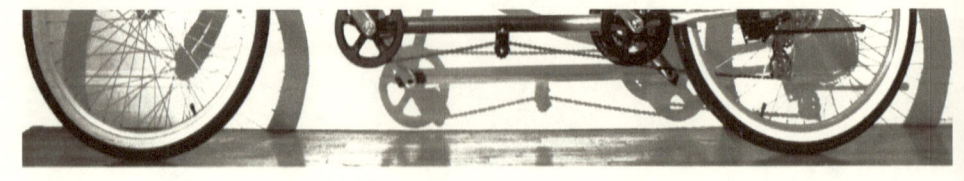

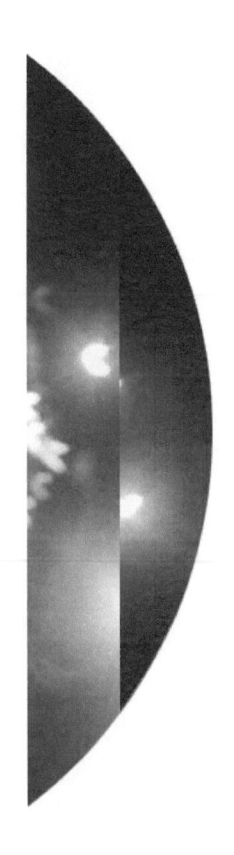

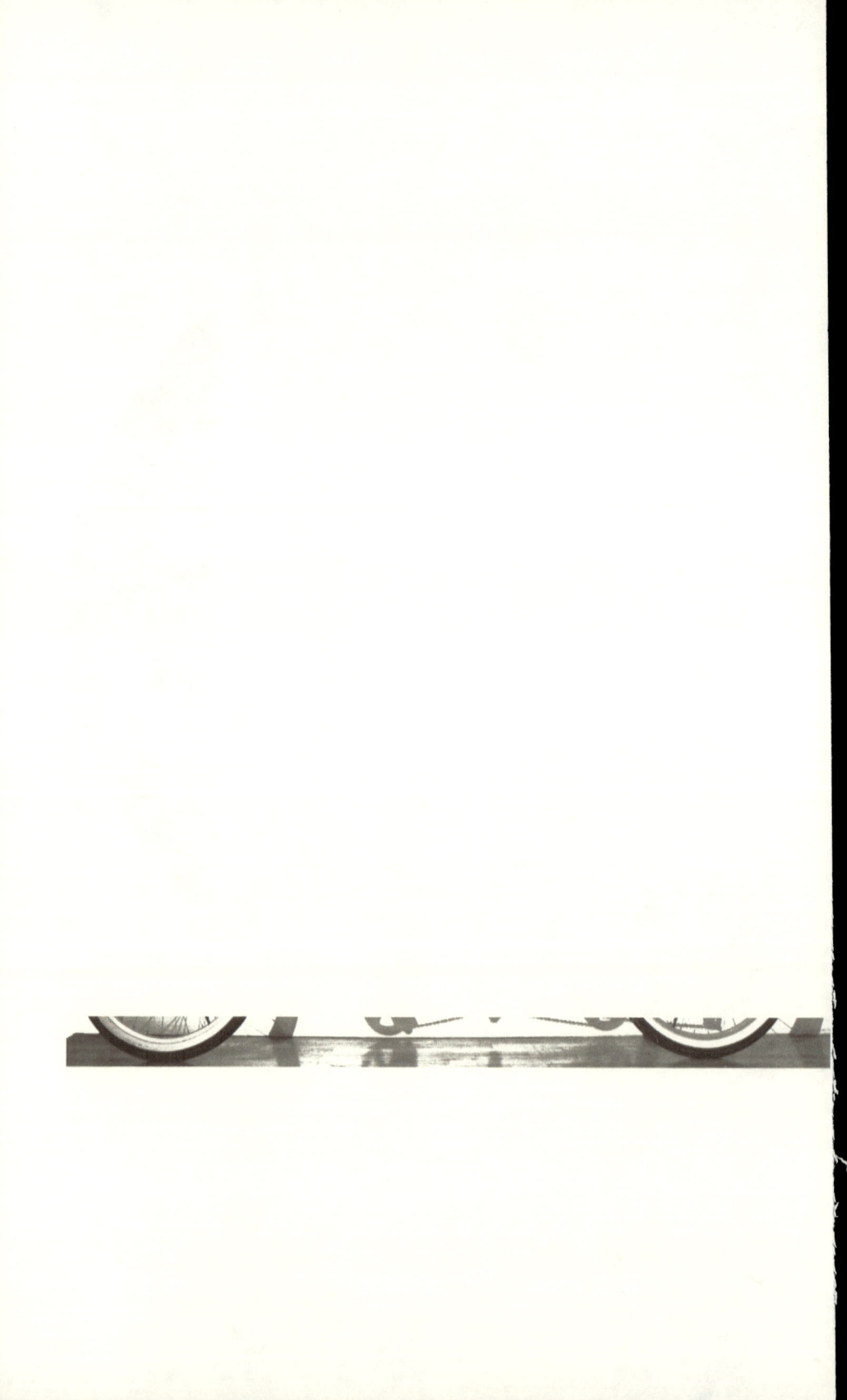

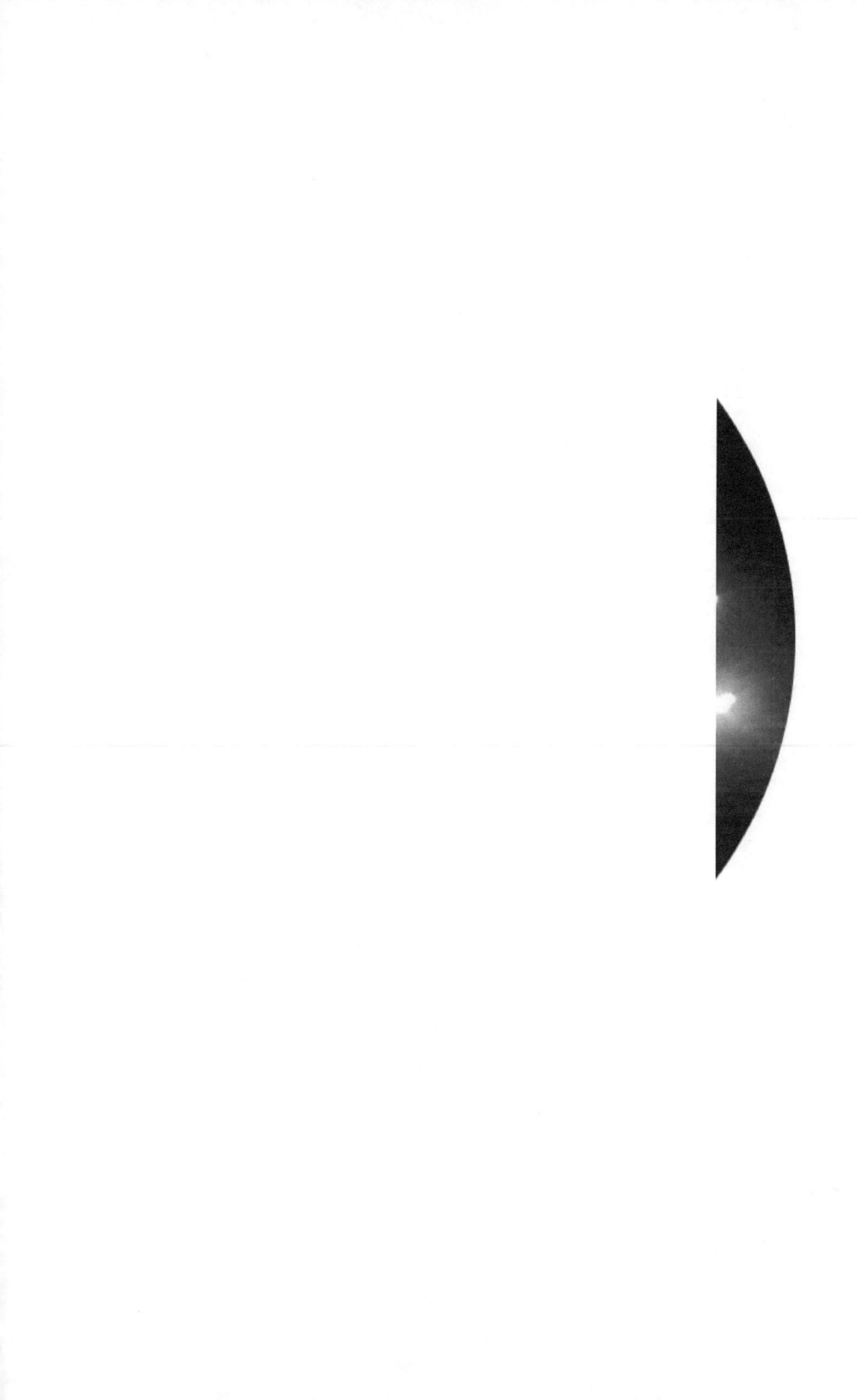

www.ingramcontent.com/pod-product-compliance
Lightning Source LLC
Chambersburg PA
CBHW022131170526
45157CB00004B/1829